WARRIOR UNLEASHED

How To Thrive In The Face
Of Uncertainty

Jennifer K. Morgan

Copyright @ 2021 Jennifer K. Morgan
www.jenniferkmorgan.com
Cover Photo: INNA's Photography
Cover Design:
Ariphotography & Luxury Branding and Design
Lighthouse Global Publishing and PR
www.lighthouseglobalinc.com

ISBN
978-1-950621-02-6 (ebook)
978-1-950621-03-3 (print)

Contents

Dedication 4

Introduction 5

CHAPTER 1
THEY CALLED ME A DREAMER TOO 11

CHAPTER 2
BORN ENTREPRENEUR 23

CHAPTER 3
WHO HAVE YOU HELPED TODAY? 39

CHAPTER 4
THE POWER OF PRAYER 51

CHAPTER 5
LEGACY 67

CHAPTER 6
DO THE RIGHT THING 81

CHAPTER 7
WITH OR WITHOUT YOU 93

CHAPTER 8
FILLING YOUR CUP 105

CHAPTER 9
LIFE ON PURPOSE 117

CHAPTER 10
DO THE HARD THING 129

CHAPTER 11
A NEW KIND OF HEALTH 143

Dedication

I dedicate this book first and foremost to my Lord and Savior Jesus Christ for blessing me with this gift which is my life, and for always being right by my side, carrying me when I needed to be carried. I give Him all the glory in Jesus' Name Amen.

I also dedicate this book to my husband, Steve, who always encourages me to do the hard thing. Thank you for being there with me always through the good times and the toughest times. I love playing and praying together. Life is so much sweeter with you in it.

To my dad and mom for raising me with the morals and values that I cherish and carry with me today.

To my sisters Sandra, Stephanie & Irene, who are my best friends and make my life so much brighter.

I love you all so much.

And to all the warriors out there, you inspire me daily. I dedicate this book to you all.

Introduction

More than anything else, I want freedom, and I am obsessed with helping others have it too. I know what it's like to feel trapped with no way out in sight. I have been to hell and back many times throughout my life. I've had dreams unravel in my hands before, relationships that left me wondering if I could ever love or trust again. I've cried out to God with faith smaller than a mustard seed. I've sat and cried alone, feeling certain that things were too messed up to fix. I've stood on the edge of financial catastrophe before, terrified because I couldn't see a way forward. I have been knocked down so hard before that I was afraid to get back up and try again.

But I always got back up, and I knew I had become stronger every time I did. It wasn't until I was diagnosed with Rheumatoid Arthritis that left me in constant pain and on really bad days, unable to get out of bed–that I found out what I'm truly capable of. Sometimes your greatest challenge can become the final ingredient to the very best version of you.

I have also had some enormous wins in life, where my hard work paid off in dividends. My life today reflects the dream life I imagined so long ago. I want people to know there is hope no matter how dark the room becomes. Even the smallest of embers can be fanned to flame. I know this because after every dark night of the soul I've experienced-the sun always rose the next day.

I have had the privilege of coaching thousands of people over the past 30 years toward becoming the best version of themselves in health, business, and life. You are not alone. You have a tribe of people all over who are waking up, refusing to settle, and determined to have real freedom.

Each chapter unfolds lessons I have learned the hard way, that could not only save you time and money but your quality of life.

I want to help you take your dreams into reality, so I've included exercises at the end of each chapter to help you reflect, gain powerful insight and then take action. I recommend reading the book in chapter order because the lessons build on each other. Thank you for showing up for me by being here, and I can't wait to show up for you!

CHAPTER 1

They Called Me a Dreamer Too

"For I know the plans I have for you," declares the Lord, "plans to prosper you and not to harm you, plans to give you hope and a future."

Jeremiah 29:11

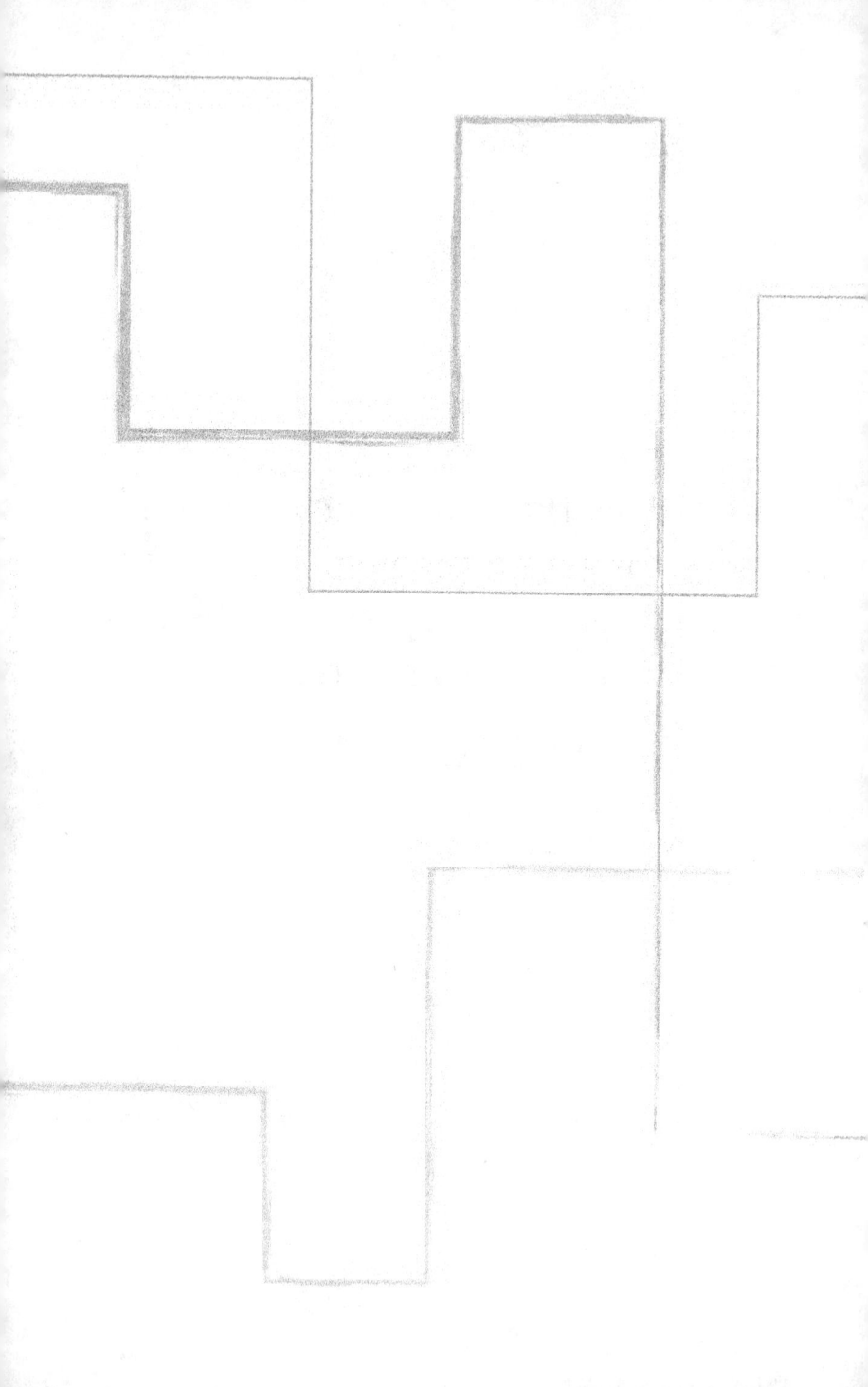

They Called Me a Dreamer Too

"For I know the plans I have for you," declares the Lord, "plans to prosper you and not to harm you, plans to give you hope and a future." - Jeremiah 29:11

I have never wanted to "fit in." I'm not sure how I dodged that bullet, but as far back as I can remember, I've carried this innate sense that I have an internal compass that I can trust. It hasn't always been easy, that's for sure, but I can say it's always been worth it.

As I sit here today in my literal dream home nestled in the foothills of Northern California, watching the sun cascade over the treetops as far as the eye can see, I feel blessed. I'm married to my best friend Steve, the love of my life, and every day I get to do what I love for a living.

It is my firm belief that if you want to be extraordinarily, successful, and fulfilled, you can be, despite any setback. I have faced more obstacles than I can count and made it through each. In fact, I have been asked so many times how I've gotten to where I am today that I decided to lay it all out for you with this book.

I am living my dream life, and I know exactly how I got here. It wasn't by accident. I am sitting here today 100% on purpose. My success is not a mystery, and to be honest, I have made it my life's work to help others win as I have.

I have had the honor of helping countless people do the same over the years, and it has proven to me time and time again that the principles I live by create a *warrior unleashed.* There is a relentless, powerful, loving force in each of us that can create anything we set our hearts and minds on when awakened.

It's easy to shrink in a world where stepping up and out can be scary. When you feel small because of the way someone has treated you or because when you've let yourself be seen and then been shut down. It's hard to want big things when even the little things aren't going right.

> I am sitting here today 100% on purpose.
>
> Jennifer K. Morgan

When I said I was okay with not fitting in, it doesn't mean it felt good to be made fun of or criticized. I felt incredibly self-conscious about how skinny I was growing up. I couldn't even express that because I was ashamed of what others saw as a genetic jackpot. I was just genetically rail-thin and towered in height over kids my age. I would often wear two pairs of pants on top of each other to try and appear less thin. I stood out whether I wanted to or not, and it's safe to say I didn't want to. I dreaded the first day of school each year when the teacher would take roll, I would literally want to crawl under my desk. As the teacher would call out each student's name to make sure they were in class, they would always pause when it came to my name. I always knew they were preparing to say my name, and I would brace myself each time. Then they would say with an unsure look on their face, "Eugenia Kapogiannis."

I would answer, "Here," and scrunch down in my seat, mortified because, well you know, kids can be mean and who has the name Eugenia Kapogiannis? It's Greek, and I am 100% Greek. By 6th grade, I changed my name to Jenny, which is my Aunt's name and my mom said Jenny is American for Eugenia, so I didn't ask questions and was happy to have a more common name. Further, I was magnetically drawn to thinking outside of the box. I was always looking for how I could figure things out more efficiently, achieve goals more quickly, and let me tell you, that is not always seen as a strength in every circle. I never excelled in school, outside of art classes and PE, it was painfully boring to me. I often found myself daydreaming, and to be honest, I was happy to pass my classes even if it meant getting a C or D. In my Junior year, I became ill for three months with Infectious Mononucleosis, more commonly known as Mono. I dropped down to 99 lbs from my already too thin 120 lbs, 5-foot 8-inch tall body and failed my Junior year because I missed an entire semester of school. I was just too sick to go. I was told that I would have to repeat my Junior year or go to a continuation school. I chose continuation school because I was too prideful to stay back a year and graduate with my little sister. In just a few short months of attending the continuation school, I knew it wasn't for me. So I made a decision to take my GED and graduate from high school early.

I was known as the black sheep in my family. I have been frightening my parents with my way of doing things differently since I hit the ground running as a toddler. My three sisters weren't even allowed to hang out with me in my teenage years because I was like the wind. I was filled with ideas, pushing back on what I didn't believe in, standing up for what I did, and really just trying to find my way on this big planet. This scared the heck out of my parents, who were conservative and fearful of my out-of-the-box thinking.

My parents often called me a dreamer, but I knew I would reach up and pull my dreams into reality. I was committed to proving to them that I could live life on my terms, which I now call a life by design. I wanted to make them proud while being true to myself. Good news… today, I believe I have done that.

When I didn't graduate from high school and got my GED instead, I still knew I was going places, but society wasn't sure about that. When I made my first million, I was certain that if I could do it, we all could. My amazing Greek family learned to brace themselves for whatever mission I was on, and today I am proud to say that they fully embrace my entrepreneurial spirit and tell me every time I talk with them that they are proud of me.

I'm hardwired to see limitations as optional, and I fully embrace that as a superpower. When I look at people, I see unlimited potential, and my first questions to anyone are: *What do you want in this life? What are you passionate about?* And *Who do you want to become?* If you can answer those questions, you are halfway there. If you want something in life, you can find a way to have it, and the person you become to achieve it will be your greatest victory. When dreamers start doing–all bets are off.

I believe we are here to help each other be the very best we can be, and each one of us has a warrior inside that wants to run free and make this world an even better place.

Our inner warrior understands her value, holds true to her faith, moves forward with courage beyond fear, fights for the best for those she loves, and shows up with every part of her that makes her unique. Our inner warrior welcomes success and helps create it for others; she knows when to say yes and when to say no, she doesn't give up, she is visionary and takes the right actions necessary not to let herself down.

We sense the warrior in each other, we have heard the call, and we know our tribe is out there and ready to play full-out in life. If you are reading this book, you are my tribe, and I am going to share with you the key principles that have given me more freedom in love, money, and life than even this big dreamer could dream. Thank you again for showing up.

> My parents often called me a dreamer, but I knew I would reach up and pull my dreams into reality.
>
> Jennifer K. Morgan

Chapter One Exercise

Take a moment to answer the following questions by freewriting your answers without overthinking them:

- *What do you want in this life?*
- *What are you passionate about?*
- *Who do you want to become?*

CHAPTER 2

Born Entrepreneur

"Be strong and courageous. Do not be afraid; do not be discouraged, for the Lord your God will be wherever you go."

Joshua 1:9

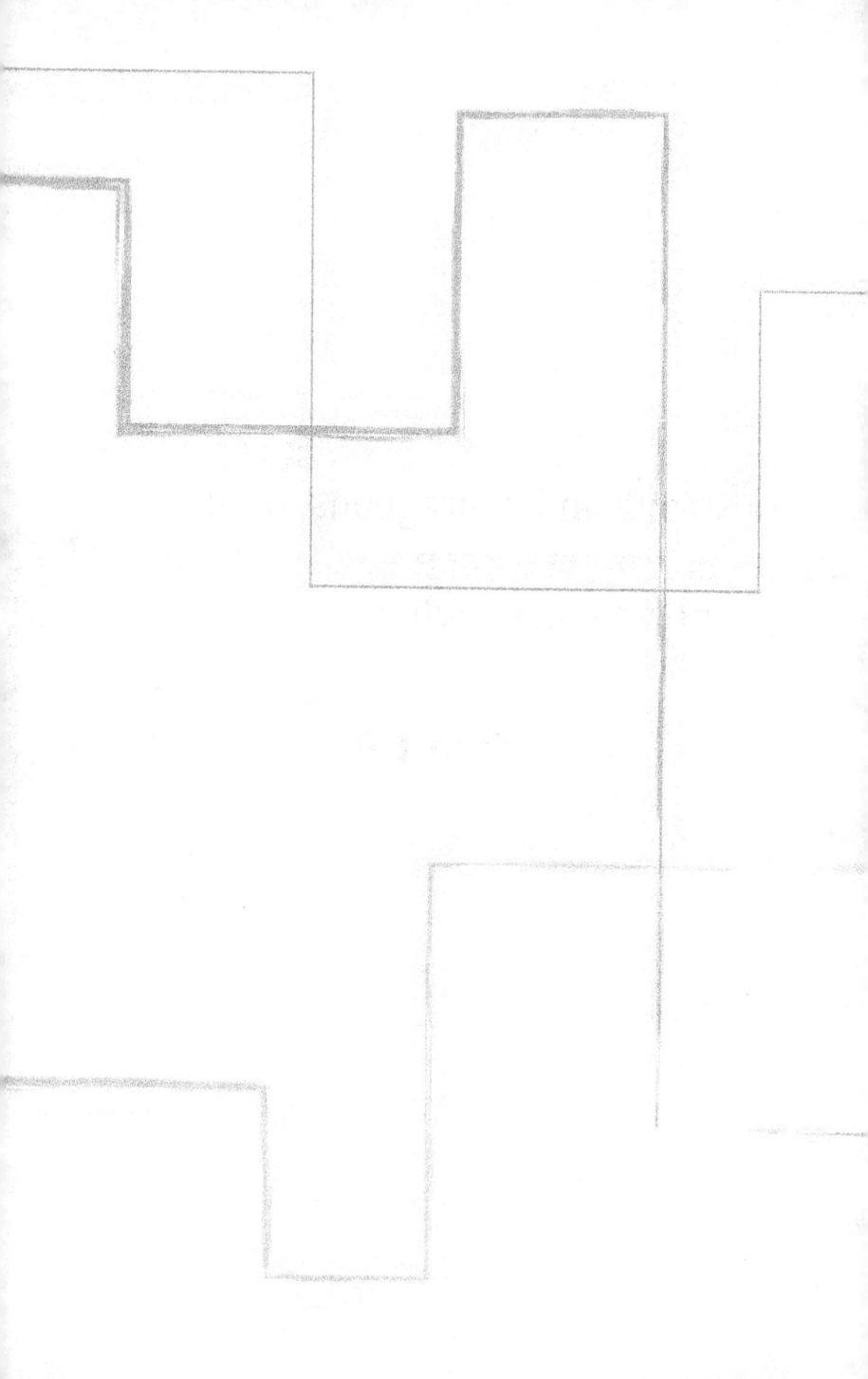

Born Entrepreneur

"Be strong and courageous. Do not be afraid; do not be discouraged, for the Lord your God will be wherever you go." - Joshua 1:9

I'm not sure if I can think of anything worse than feeling trapped, stuck in a life or circumstance that you feel powerless to escape. Being an entrepreneur comes with many benefits, but the greatest, in my opinion, is freedom.

Entrepreneurs have this voice inside of them that says, "You are responsible for your destiny; it's up to you to make it happen." There is nothing wrong with a 9-5 job working for someone else if it makes you happy, but I knew early on it just wasn't for me. I always loved that quote by Jim Rohn, "Work hard at your job, and you can make a living. Work hard on yourself, and you can make a fortune." I always had a job but I was always working towards a project on the side and working on myself to one day make a fortune.

I wanted to have control over how much money I made, how I spent it, how often I could travel, who I spent my time with, and where my time went. It always came down to freedom. Freedom to live life on my terms, I had to have independence to have freedom. I also wanted to make sure that I loved what I did every single day, and I knew early on that I loved helping people.

We didn't have a lot of money growing up for non-essentials, meaning if I wanted new clothes or the newest & trendy shoes, it was a hardship. My mom was an amazing seamstress and made my sisters and me all of our clothes and bows for our hair when we were little. Although money was tight, we never went without what we needed. My parents worked hard and taught me what a strong work ethic looked like and the importance of saving money for a rainy day. My dad and mom often told me that money doesn't grow on trees and if I wanted something extra beyond a roof over my head, food on the table, and clothes on my back, then I needed to be prepared to work for it, this included any special education that I wanted to take part in and my future car. I saved a portion of every paycheck and was able to buy my first car. I knew I wanted to travel, and understanding the value of budgeting made it possible for me to begin traveling young. When I paid for my first trip to Hawaii at just 18 years old, I fell in love with traveling and have prioritized it ever since. My dad also taught me the importance of having good credit and encouraged me to build my own credit by getting a credit card and making small purchases that I could pay off monthly. Thanks to my dad, today, my credit score is over 825.

My dad also told me that as soon as I turned 18 that I would be paying rent at home. Simply put, my dad made me a hustler. I used to think he was too tough on my sisters and me, but I know today it's what made me and my sisters all hard workers. He did us all a favor. He helped us find our independence. My dad and mom's philosophy was "there are no free lunches," and you know what? It's true! Today my sisters and I thank my parents for loving us enough not to enable us. I honestly don't think I would be the person I am today without their guidance.

You are responsible for your destiny;
it's up to you to make it happen.

Jennifer K. Morgan

I couldn't wait to make my own money, and I always respected that my parents supported me in that desire.

I figured out how to get a job when I was barely old enough to work. Burger King gave me my first opportunity to start creating independence for myself. I was so excited when I learned that I had gotten the job. I didn't see "work" as most do. It wasn't something I *had* to do; I *got* to do it. It was a stepping stone toward freedom. Receiving my first paycheck felt like a million bucks because I knew it was mine, that I had earned it, and I could make decisions about what I wanted to do with it.

I was very young, so of course, I bought things like clothes, the newest gadgets, games or the latest style of shoes but it felt incredible to want something and have a way to get it for myself. I didn't have to ask or wait for anyone else to buy what I wanted. I felt independent and free.

Waiting on another person to make your dreams come true is not only risky and saturated with feelings of powerlessness, it doesn't make sense. It's irrational. It only makes sense to ask people for permission to have what your heart desires and then wait to see if they will get it for you when you are a child. Waiting on someone else to make our lives better sounds like torture to most entrepreneurs, and I have always felt like that, that's how I know I was a born entrepreneur.

How many adult people do you know that feel stuck professionally, financially, or in general who complain

BORN ENTREPRENEUR

and blame where they are in life on other people or circumstance? Have you ever tried to help someone who is stuck but won't take any of your advice? It's maddening and heartbreaking to want to help those that refuse to help themselves. I have found that the people who genuinely want freedom are actively looking for answers and find the right people to lead them to their next step.

Mentorship is one of the most valuable strategies to build your dreams and has played a fundamental role in my success. I believe behind every great entrepreneur is a great mentor.

My Uncle Nick opened my eyes as a young seeker of freedom. As a young girl just twelve years old, I was mesmerized by my Uncle Nick. I can remember his license plate on his beautiful black car that read FGREEK, it stood for Fabulous Greek, and he was the first entrepreneur I had a front-row seat to learn from. He lived in a huge beautiful home with a beautiful backyard and pool surrounded by life-size white greek statues in the Oakland Hills in the Bay Area of California. Uncle Nick was an entrepreneur and owned a restaurant in Oakland near Lake Merritt and a restaurant/bar in San Francisco.

He walked with confidence, head always held high, big gold chain necklaces, always happy and smiling, he looked like a movie star. He also had very nice things, was always traveling, and always seemed to be enjoying life. But more than any of the above, something really stood out to me:

He had a Personal Assistant.

Most people clean their own house & cook their own meals. It's a normal part of life, but Uncle Nick was able to hire other people to clean his house, and when he would have holiday gatherings or parties, there was always someone that would help with the cooking and serving food. He and my Aunt Nancy were free to visit with me and the rest of the guests. He was able to be present with us all instead of running around taking care of all of the logistics. I saw it was possible to create a life where you could decide what you do and don't want to do with your time. I didn't mind cleaning or hard work. It wasn't about having a personal assistant, it was about having the *option* of having one. Uncle Nick's life was filled with options, and he had the freedom to choose his schedule, his quality of life, and his destiny. He showed me what I already knew in my heart, *we have the power to create the life we choose.* I knew then I would have my own businesses one day. I didn't realize it at the time because I was too young, but my Uncle Nick, in essence, was one of my first great mentors. Oh, how I wish he were alive today to tell him what an impact he had on me. I would love to let him know he was one of my first great mentors.

I was in my mid 20's when I started my first of many successful companies. I loved the beauty industry and was able to get my 24/7 tanning services offered inside of a local gym in Modesto, California. I had also become a licensed manicurist a few years prior, so I was able to offer tanning and nails in the same location. I had also become a personal trainer by this time and had a growing clientele. These all provided recurring revenue and scalability without a large overhead. I was just getting my feet wet, but I was off to a great start. Many people I knew my age were still either in school or limbo, wondering what they were going to do with their lives, and I was already creating mine.

It was during this season I met a mentor who completely changed my life. Dr. Chet Graham owned two chiropractic clinics in my area, and one was located inside of the gym where I ran my business. I would watch how he lived his life, ran his practices, and treated people–I was amazed. He would get more done in a single day than I knew possible. Further, he took excellent care of his health no matter how busy he was, even while building his own dream home with his bare hands on the side. He saw how hard I was working as a young entrepreneur. He offered me excellent advice on business, revenue streams, client retention and growth, personal growth and helped lay the foundation for my vast knowledge of nutrition and health I have today. He was willing to take me under his wing and share the keys to the kingdom with me, but I had to show up and take the action. He had a truly remarkable impact on my life, and after meeting him, I had the courage to go much bigger in business. I have always considered Dr. Graham not only a mentor but a dear friend. Although I have told Dr. Graham and his beautiful wife Robin what a remarkable impact they've made in my life over the years, they may never fully know how grateful I am for their continued friendship and mentorship. I think it's important to let the people who have inspired you throughout your life know that they have because it's common that we have no idea how we've impacted others.

All this to say, seek out mentorship to be inspired and grow. I think the minute you believe you know everything is the minute you know nothing. To have a great mentor, you must be will to be a great mentee.

Over the years, I have worked with so many people inside my companies, on my teams, attending conferences, etc., and I noticed 3 types of people walk through the door: A-Players, B-Players, and C-Players; two of the three can make excellent mentees.

A-Players have designated themselves as 100% responsible for the outcome of their life. They don't wait for permission to find solutions to problems that need solving. They find the resources necessary to move the needle forward. They ask for help if they need it and ask questions unapologetically. A-Players are often entrepreneurs, company owners, founders, CEOs, and managers. The buck usually stops with them, meaning they don't shift blame, and they proactively do what it takes to ensure success. A-Players create the kind of life with options, move things forward, and go above and beyond when necessary.

People who genuinely want freedom are actively looking for answers and find the right people to lead them to their next step.

Jennifer K. Morgan

B-Players take responsibility for getting things done. They do what is asked, no more, no less. They aren't going to come up with innovative solutions, but they will implement what is requested. They are dependable and can keep things stable. B-Players are great employees. They aren't going to change the world, but they aren't going to let it fall apart either. Their life might feel status quo, but mitigating risk feels better than coloring too far outside the lines and risking it all. B-Players would rather guarantee a *good* outcome than leap for an uncertain *great* outcome. I have seen many B-Players become A-Players through mentorship combined with their desire to grow.

C-Players complain the most about their circumstances while taking the least amount of action to change things. C-Players can tell you why they're stuck and who's fault it is. They do the bare minimum, just enough to stay afloat. C-Players are the people who will suck the energy out of you if you try to help them when they ask for help. There is a difference between asking for help and asking for someone else to save you. C-Players don't take responsibility for how their life is turning out. They can often be spotted inside your company or life by identifying where large amounts of your time and energy are going with the least amount of return. It sounds harsh, but really, it's just fact-you can't help someone who does not want to grow.

I love people and believe there is a warrior in each of us that desires great things in this world, but not everyone is ready to level-up and do what it takes. I surround myself with A-Players and motivated B-Players as friends, mentors, business partners, mentees, and top leaders in my organizations. These are the people I invest my time, energy, and trust in. It doesn't mean I don't value or care about C-Players, I just know from hard-learned lessons that C's don't want what I have to offer and when they do, they find me.

I have to assume if you picked up my book and are still reading, you are an A-Player or a motivated B-Player, and we have found each other in divine perfect timing. You are giving your warrior permission to speak up and be free of perceived limitations. Playing small has exhausted you, and you're ready to pull out all the stops. You've come to the right place!

Chapter Two Exercise

Take a moment to answer the following question as honestly as possible:

- What, if anything, do you feel has stopped you from up-leveling your life in the past?

- How important is it to you to up-level your life now?

- Describe what kind of mentorship you've had and what type of mentorship you now believe you would benefit from.

CHAPTER 3

Who Have You Helped Today?

"Encourage one another and build each other up."

Thessalonians 5:11

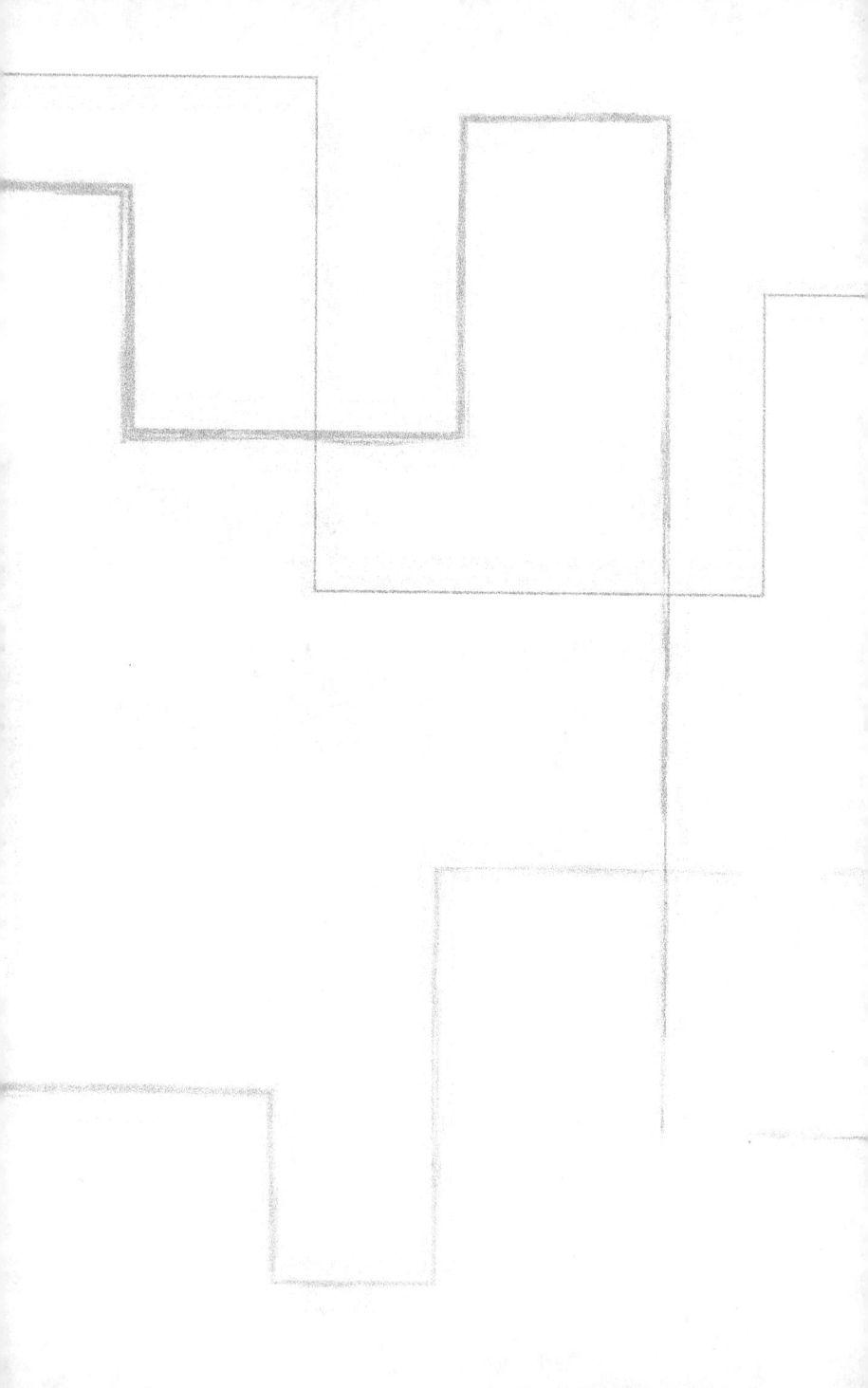

Who Have You Helped Today?

"Encourage one another and build each other up."
- 1Thessalonians 5:11

Here is an interesting thing about my success, for me, it's only really come about through helping other people become successful too. Yes, I have always set goals for myself and taken action to achieve each goal, but there wasn't a single achievement that satisfied me as deeply as helping someone else reach their goals. If success were like breathing, achievement would be the inhale, and fulfillment would be the exhale. Achievement without fulfillment isn't sustainable. I believe we are designed to help each other, offering our strengths to move everyone forward who wants to. It is essential that what I do with my life makes a difference. If it's not based on significant work, it all feels meaningless.

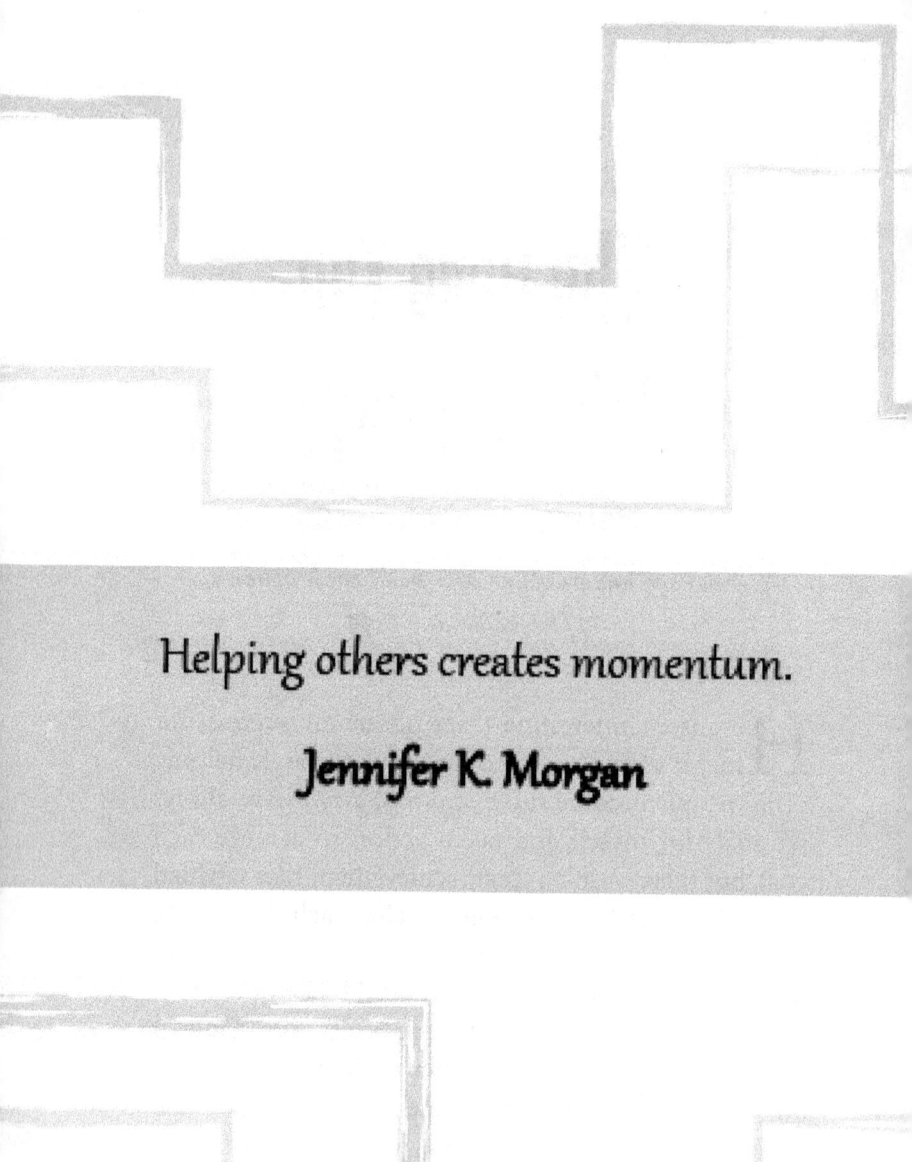

Helping others creates momentum.

Jennifer K. Morgan

A few years ago, I was able to help retire my husband from our landscape company that we owned and operated for over 14 years and was able to nearly pay off our over 7 figure home, cars, all our credit cards, plus all of our bills for the following year. I had always had a goal to be debt-free. I think debt-free is the new rich. It was one of the greatest achievements I'd experienced. It symbolized the achievement of freedom that I had worked so hard for and paved the way for me to dream an even bigger dream. The feelings that came up for me were breathtaking, but something else took place around the same time that felt even better.

A wife and mom of three young children, Shannon was introduced to me by a good friend of mine. I had asked my friend to introduce me to her when I saw her and her family featured on the cover of a local neighborhood magazine. I was looking for my next family to help and something about Shannon with her beautiful family and two Great Danes Dogs on this magazine cover stood out to me. My good friend worked for the magazine and was happy to introduce me to Shannon. When I met Shannon, she came to me in a tight spot. Her heater had broken, and she needed to make money as soon as possible to fix it. You see, Shannon and her husband Frank were in the process of adopting their son and had an in-home inspection only to learn that her heater was putting out toxic fumes. The inspector cut the wires to the heater leaving Shannon and her family with no heat. It was December, the dead of winter and cold in Shannons' home. Two weeks after I had my initial meet-up with Shannon, she came to me and asked if I could show her how to earn an additional stream of income to help pay for her new heater. I said yes, I was able to help, and she said that she was ready to do whatever it took. Shannon could have borrowed the money from a relative, but she didn't want to, and taking out a bank loan wasn't an option. Shannon felt trapped. She was fed up with worrying about how she could help provide for her children while living with the stress that she and Frank were one unexpected bill away from financial catastrophe. She wanted freedom for her family.

When Shannon exceeded her initial goal she had set out to make within the first 60 days, we were both overjoyed with tears. We celebrated with a dinner out at one of her and Frank's favorite restaurants, there were smiles and tears because I was so proud of her, and she was just so happy. I knew the sense of empowerment she felt becoming the kind of provider she had always wanted to be. Today, Shannon is highly successful in business and life and an inspiration to many. Her life today looks so much different than her life did when I first met her. Shannon is an amazing leader, she is a warrior, and today I consider Shannon one of my dearest friends.

Helping Shannon was my exhale. Nothing compares to the feelings I have when I am able to contribute to something bigger than myself. Tony Robbins said it perfectly, "Success without fulfillment is the greatest failure." All of the achievement and money would fall flat in the end if it only served me.

In the last three decades, I have had the honor of helping thousands of people like Shannon move the needle toward their own dreams, and it has, in turn, made my dreams come true.

There was nothing that could stand in the way of me reaching my goals because my goals were tied to my deepest values.

Jennifer K. Morgan

Helping others creates momentum.

Motivation isn't sustainable when it is based on money alone. I have always wanted to make a lot of money, and through hard work, discipline, and dedication, I am doing great. The truth, however, is it was never about the money. I was crystal clear on what the money would give me. I wanted the freedom and independence to be able to help as many people as possible and create an extraordinary life of adventure for my family and me. This was worth getting out of bed and jumping through any fire for. There was nothing that could stand in the way of me reaching my goals because my goals were tied to my deepest values. This kind of motivation has an endless fuel source that doesn't fizzle out in the face of adversity.

Shannon's goal wasn't really to make enough money for a new heater, her goal wasn't even to keep her family warm, it was deeper than even that. Shannon's goal was to become the person who could contribute and help give her family safety from the hardship of struggle and the freedom to give her children the best chance at a remarkable life. Further, today Shannon helps other people achieve their goals as I did with her.

Helping others is a gift that keeps on giving and one of the most powerful paths to creating wealth for you and those around you.

Chapter Three Exercise

Think about the last time you helped someone or locked arms with others to achieve a goal bigger than yourself. Take a moment to answer the following questions:

- Describe what you feel when you've helped someone else.

- Now think about what you do for a living and see where you could create more of that feeling in how you make money. Think about how you could attach your financial goals to something greater than yourself.

CHAPTER 4

The Power of Prayer

"I can do all things through Christ who gives me strength."

Philippians 4:13

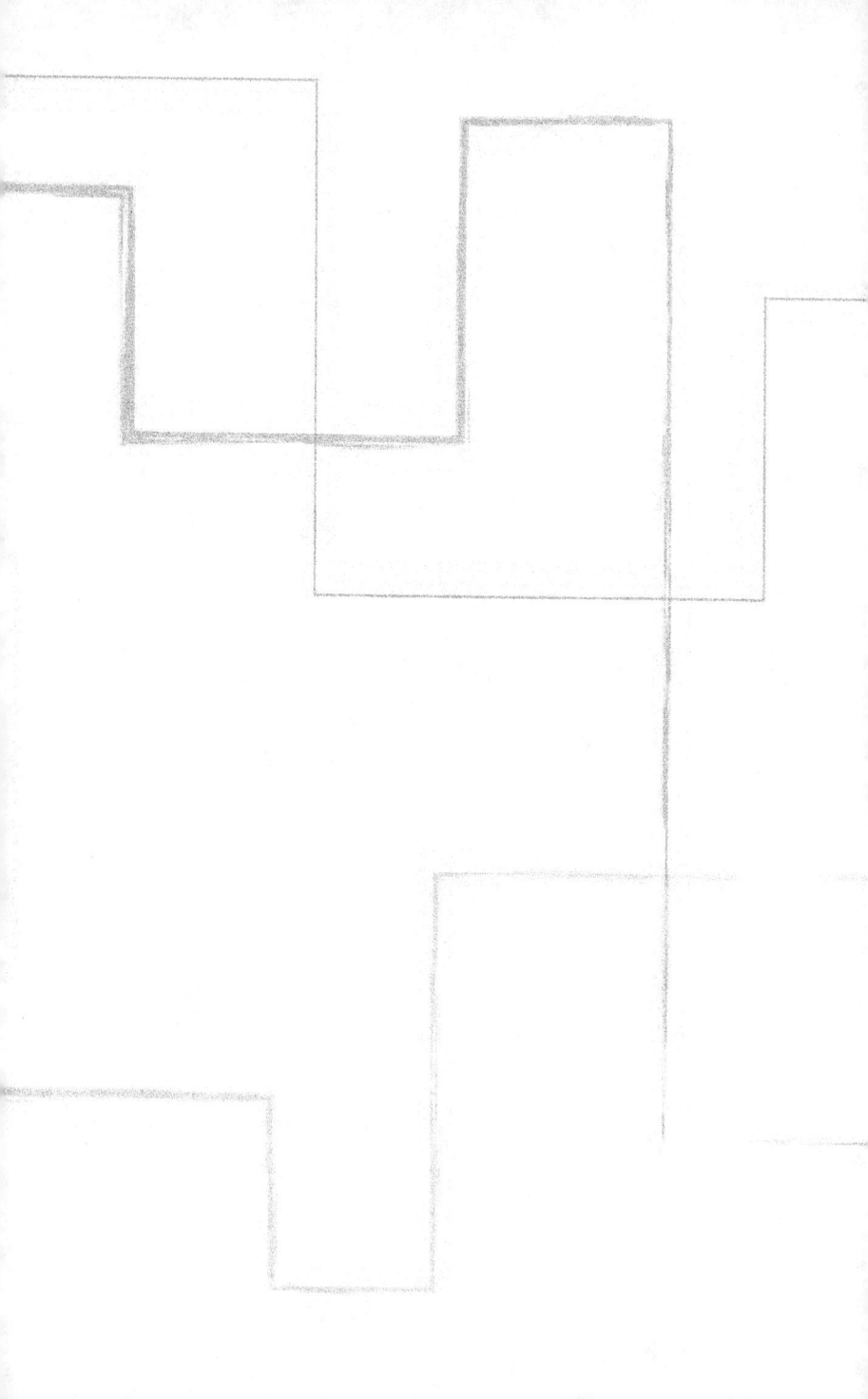

The Power of Prayer

"I can do all things through Christ who gives me strength" Philippians 4:13

I knew something was off with my health for some time. My energy had dropped, my body was aching, it felt like not being able to fully recharge a battery no matter how hard I tried. The confusing part, I was one of the healthiest people I knew, or so I should have been. I had just turned 50, and I had been working out, eating healthy, taking vitamins, spending time in nature, and I had always had faith in God, but something was happening to my health, and deep down, I knew I couldn't ignore it.

I began to experience pain that would burn and ache through my body, specifically my joints that would radiate out, making it hard to take a shower, get dressed, and tie my own shoes. One of the most devastating things was how hard it became for me to play with my dogs and go on hikes, two things that I loved to do most with my husband. I had built a career in health and wellness professionally. I even competed in a bikini fitness competition in my 30's and had been featured in several fitness magazines over the course of a decade. The first large company I co-owned was a Gold's Gym in Modesto, California, health had always been prioritized in my life, and suddenly I could barely work out, and when I did, I hurt so badly the next day it felt like my body was hit with a baseball bat. None of it made any sense to me. Everything seemed more difficult to do. Even small tasks like opening water bottles became more and more challenging. I often used my teeth or asked for help from my husband. I found it harder and harder to get out of bed in the morning, which was sad for me because I cherished my mornings. I had always been a morning person, it was my favorite time of the day. But this was so unlike any pain I had ever experienced, it was life-changing pain.

I was terrified.

I went to Doctor after Doctor and had countless tests to get to the bottom of my rapid health decline. My blood work always came back perfect. The Doctors dismissed me because I looked so healthy. They thought I had anxiety and tried to medicate me, which I refused. I decided to become my own advocate by researching, asking questions, and building strong relationships with the Integrative Doctors I found that could take into consideration all of the symptoms that had presented and diagnose and treat accordingly.

I had been diagnosed with Hashimoto's, an autoimmune disease that attacks your thyroid 16 years prior, but that was kept under control with medication and a healthy diet. Without question, something was terribly wrong, and I knew I had to do everything possible to get to the bottom of it. I was willing to take drastic action to regain my health. Shortly after I began sharing the symptoms I was experiencing with people close to me, I had several mention that my breast implants could be contributing to my health decline. I had gotten breast implants 23 years prior, I chose saline implants because it just made sense to me from a safety standpoint. Until that time, I hadn't heard of any serious health concerns related to having the procedure.

I had been to my Doctor, who had put my implants in for regular checkups over 23 years of having them; each visit, I was told everything was in perfect shape. I began to research the possibility of the onset of illness post breast augmentation. Much to my shock, I right away found countless articles and case studies correlating both saline and silicone breast implants with countless illnesses appearing in women post-surgery, many of which were auto-immune diseases. I found a forum on Facebook where I read hundreds of women's testimonies of the illnesses that presented after they had implants. I could not believe how many of them had both Hashimoto's and RA, along with countless other symptoms and diseases. What really stood out to me was how many were like me, completely healthy prior and with no family history of the symptoms or illnesses that presented after their surgeries. Known symptoms of Breast Implant Illness are far too many to list here but to give you a few: rashes, memory loss, brain fog, depression, anxiety, joint pain, muscle pain, sinus congestion, vertigo, premature aging, IBS symptoms, connective tissue disorder symptoms, fibromyalgia symptoms, body inflammation, enlarged lymph nodes, Autoimmune diseases and so many more. Many women present with a myriad of awful symptoms following breast augmentation and never even receive a diagnosis for something specific.

Prayer became my lifeline, the silver cord I held in my hands to guide me through when I couldn't see the light with my eyes but only feel it with my heart.

Jennifer K. Morgan

Was it my implants that caused my health decline? I will never know for sure, I just knew in my spirit it was time for me to take them out of my body. Here's what I do know, after extensive research, I learned there are over 40 plus toxic chemicals and heavy metals that the implant shell and filling alone is comprised of: formaldehyde, lead-based solder, phenol, heavy metals, lacquer thinner, and Toluene to name a just a few. Clearly, this couldn't be good for my body or my health. Further, after having an allergy and sensitivity test it showed that I have a severe allergy/sensitivity to both Toluene and formaldehyde. Really I just had to put two and two together. I recalled about two years following my breast augmentation, I began to have panic attacks. I had never had them before, and further, I rarely felt anxiety, yet I would just suddenly have a panic attack. I began experiencing a significant amount of those symptoms related to Breast Implant Illness and was eventually diagnosed with Hashimoto's autoimmune disorder. Keep in mind, I was then and now one of the most healthy people I knew. Minus a few years in my late 20's, early 30's of weekend warrior nights out (which come Monday, I went right back to my healthy eating and workouts), I truly took care of my body. I believe having two foreign objects in my body, which my body was always fighting as foreign objects, had to have caused problems. It's kind of like when your finger has a splinter, the area becomes red and inflamed as your body attempts to push it out, knowing it doesn't belong there. It began to all make sense to me. I decided to have my implants removed immediately. On November 5th, 2019, an explant specialist removed them, and I felt lighter with less back pain almost immediately. The difference in my health would take time following the removal of my implants. I knew to reclaim my health, it might take months or years. I was up for the challenge then, and I'm up for it now. It is a process that I take on every day. There was a small part of me that wondered if I would miss them after they were gone. It turns out I felt more attractive and comfortable in my own body than I had before. My concern at this point was my health, with very little focus on what anyone else would think. It felt so good to have them out of my body and moving towards regaining my health. When I shared, I was having implant removal for health reasons, I had an enormous amount of love and support from the people I care about and even from Doctors. My goal today is to educate others regarding the potential risks of breast augmentation so others might have the opportunity to make an informed decision. I was so young when I had gotten mine, thinking they would make me feel better about my body being skinny and for bikini/fitness photos and competitions. I had no idea that I needed to do my due diligence because so many people had them, and the Doctors made no mention that my health could be adversely affected for years to come. Every *body* is different. I wholeheartedly think my body responded very negatively to my breast implants, and over 140,000 women in a FB group page that I am a part of feel the same way. However, there are many people who seem to be fine. Again, my primary reason for sharing my body's reaction to having implants is that I would have loved someone to warn me about the potential side effects to have made a fully informed decision for my health. The Hashimotos was just the beginning; the following diagnosis was the one that explained why my body was in such debilitating pain.

This new pain and new diagnosis that I finally received in 2019 was Rheumatoid Arthritis (RA).

My own body's immune system was attacking its own tissues. The lining surrounding my joints (synovial membrane) was becoming inflamed and thickened, and fluid was building up, causing swelling, erosion, and degradation of my joints and tissue. A deeper dive into some specific blood work confirmed this. I was crushed and felt sad, frustrated, and angry. I had spent most of my life working out, eating healthy, taking my supplements, and doing everything I could do to stay on point with living a healthy lifestyle. It just didn't seem fair.

The physical pain was almost more than I could bear at times, but the psychological pain had the potential to take me out completely.

The power of being in constant conversation with my heavenly father has increased my faith, made the impossible possible, and shown me firsthand that we are more supported than we may ever fully understand.

Jennifer K. Morgan

I had lived my life up until this point with freedom and momentum that filled my days with activity, travel, team building, interaction, movement in mind, body, and spirit that was exciting and meaningful–and suddenly, the only time I wasn't in pain was when I was asleep in bed, and even that reprieve was slipping away.

Enormous questions arose about who I was and what might become of me without my health? This time in my life ripped through the fabric of who I believed I was and where I believed my strength had come from.

To the outside world, I remained as positive and optimistic as humanly possible, and on really bad days, which there were plenty, my husband Steve handled the frontlines of our companies.

I was in the fight of my life. I wasn't just fighting for my health; I was fighting for hope.

No matter what was happening with my body, I knew that I had to tap into something greater than my body that could see me through this dark valley.

I knew I had a warrior spirit, but this was the first time I had been in a battle that required every piece of armor if I was going to make it out, standing tall.

Prayer became my lifeline, the silver cord I held in my hands to guide me through when I couldn't see the light with my eyes but only feel it with my heart.

I can do all things through Christ who strengthens me (Philippians 4:13).

I had known this verse for years, but these words became the lamp unto my feet. Every morning I woke in prayer, spent the day praying, and fell asleep praying.

I can't speak of what prayer is to anyone else, but for me, it is the most intimate, powerful relationship I share with my creator. It sounds like speaking from my heart to my most trusted partner on earth and beyond.

I believe the tongue has the power of life and death (Proverbs 18:21). What I speak over my body, my health, my business, my everything— matters. In prayer when I say, "I can do all things through Christ who strengthens me." It is so. When I wake up and thank God for taking care of all the people in my life and express my profound gratitude for a new day and all the blessings that come with it, it is so. Life represents the light, growth, hope, healing, moving forward, or highest potential for good in any circumstance, even illness. Death is the negativity, worst-case scenario, contraction, hopelessness, more disease, giving up on what could be.

I choose to speak life, and the power of prayer has never been more clear to me than it is today. I have gained a new level of health that I had not known prior to leaning into prayer as I have. I will unpack this in the last chapter of this book. However, I can say this— although I still have some pain, I am happy to say that my RA is 80% in remission, working towards 100%

and mentally along with spiritually, I have never been healthier than I am today.

The power of being in constant conversation with my heavenly father has increased my faith, made the impossible possible, and shown me firsthand that we are more supported than we may ever fully understand. Faith is the bedrock I have built my proverbial house on, and prayer gives me the strength and courage to transcend any limitation that has shown its face to me with grace. I have become a warrior unleashed.

Thank you to my family and friends who have prayed for me and continue to pray for me during some of my darkest, most painful moments.

Chapter 4 Exercise

Take a moment and reflect on how faith has played a role in your life. In times of uncertainty, it's common to want to contract and not act in life. Faith can help us take action even when we are afraid and don't have all of the answers.

- Name at least 3 areas in your life right now that you feel like you need to take action but feel too afraid of the uncertainty.

- Now commit those 3 areas to prayer every day for the next 30 days.

- After 30 days, see if you can see all of the miracles! This will not only reinforce the power of prayer but increase your faith which will give you the ability to have peace beyond all understanding.

CHAPTER 5

Legacy

"May the God of hope fill you with all joy and peace as you trust in him, so that you may overflow with hope by the power of the Holy Spirit."

Romans 15:13

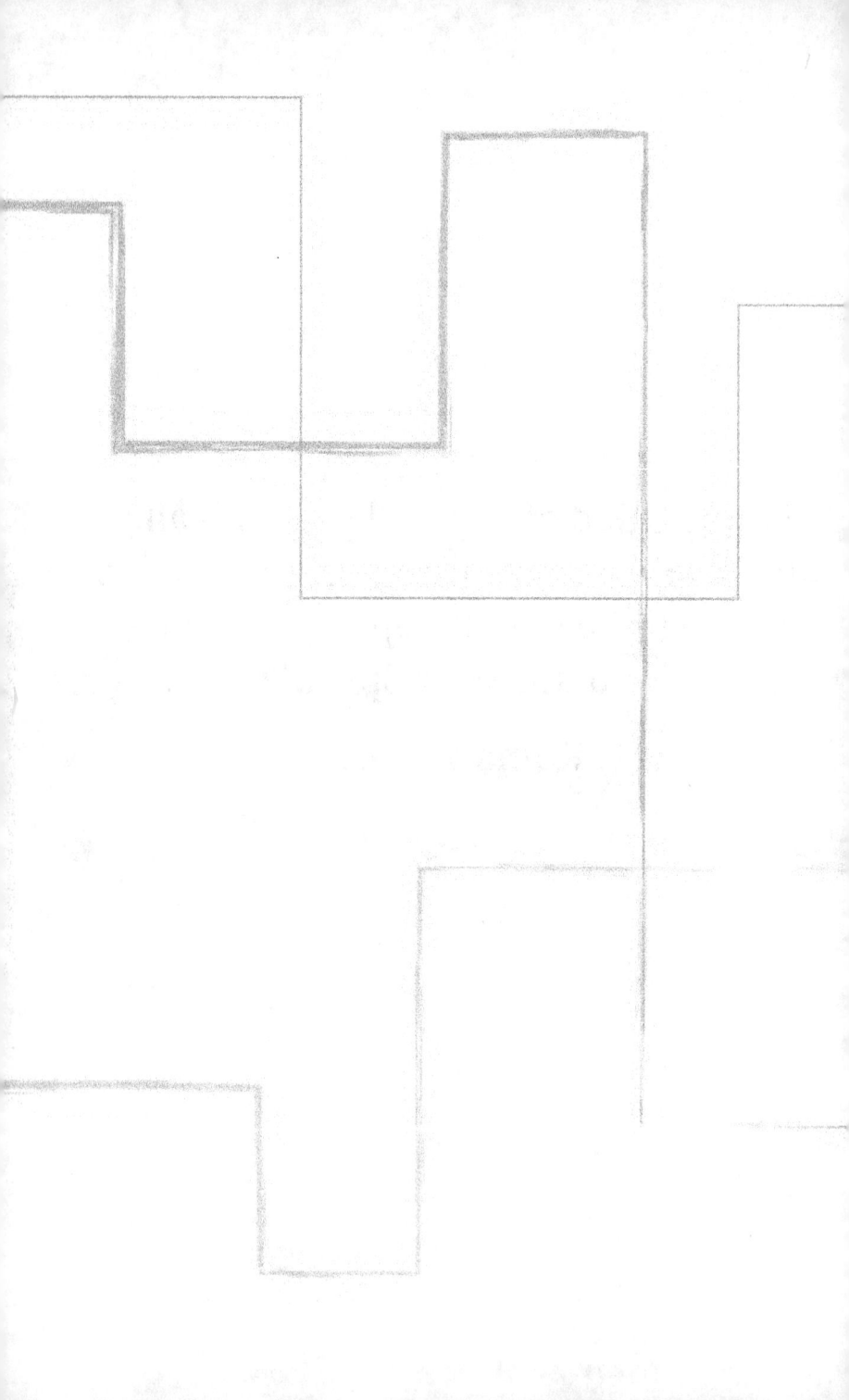

Legacy

'May the God of hope fill you with all joy and peace as you trust in him, so that you may overflow with hope by the power of the Holy Spirit.' - Romans 15:13

Start in the beginning with the end in mind. I love adventure and experiencing wonderful new things in life. In fact, the first time I had ever traveled, I went to Hawaii and loved it so much I went back two weeks later. I was only 18-years-old at the time, and I have gone back several times since. Today, one of my favorite places to travel to is Cabo San Lucas, Mexico. I guess it's because it was the first vacation that my husband Steve and I had taken together when we first met, and it's where we fell in love. We have traveled there at least once or twice a year since then. Cabo holds a very special place in my heart. This year when we celebrated our 10-year wedding anniversary Steve and I renewed our vows in Cabo. Just the two of us. It was so special and just another reason why Cabo will always be so special to us.

Making it to Cabo every year for almost a decade and recently looking into the eyes of my best friend and actual man of my dreams recommitting our love there while overlooking the ocean–isn't luck. It's part of my legacy, and I make decisions that create this life, so when I look back at the end of this road on earth, I know I made it count.

Legacy is what you leave behind after you're gone. The way you made people feel, the relationships you built, the difference you made, it's your contribution to humanity in some way.

People often don't want to think or talk about legacy because it forces the topic of mortality, and further, it holds us accountable for the life we are living. When we ask ourselves what will I leave behind then we have to look at how we are living. This is overwhelming for many and the idea of legacy doesn't hit until it's just too late to go back and do it differently.

Legacy happens either by default or design.

One of the hardest things I can imagine is coming to the end of my life and feeling regret when it's too late to do anything about it. It's said that the great regret expressed by people on their deathbed is that they wish they would have lived the life they really wanted and not the one they felt like they had to. Legacy by default can be devastating for some.

Legacy by design happens when you decide in advance what you want to see when you look back on your life and what you want to leave behind.

Legacy happens either by default or design. Legacy by design happens when you decide in advance what you want to see when you look back on your life and what you want to leave behind.

Jennifer K. Morgan

I decided years ago that I wanted my legacy to be that I lived a significant life by making a difference in this world for the better. I knew I wanted someday when I'm gone for people that I helped to be helping others. I wanted to be remembered for believing in people and their dreams, leading by example that God loves them and there is always hope. I wanted to live a life so full of possibilities that it might inspire others to live their lives to the fullest.

It's so important to have perspective and clarity about the big picture for yourself because it will inform what decisions you make on a day-to-day basis so, in the end, you have no regrets.

I wanted to help people in a significant way, so I have spent years helping others build a business and gain financial independence.

I have fanned any flame that has come near me when it comes to others' dreams because I want them to know they can do it! Whatever "it" is.

I don't just tell people about God's love; I show them by loving them without judgment.

I live the life of my dreams, travel the world, married the most incredible man. I love my beautiful bonus daughters Kaitlynn and Haley with all of my heart; they bring me so much joy. I wasn't able to have children, God had other plans. He knew they were perfectly what I needed. Their sweet spirits and incredible faith in the Lord have spoken volumes to me. I am so grateful.

I'm crazy about my new granddaughter Haven, I have an incredible loving mother-in-law who also has a warrior spirit. I'm blessed with a wonderful father, mother, 3 amazing sisters, nieces, and nephews. My sister Stephanie has been a huge inspiration in my life. She lives with Achalasia, and if you don't know what it is, you can google it. It's awful. However, when you meet her, you would never know anything was wrong. She is always smiling, and she runs 7-8 miles a day. She is my inspiration, she is beautiful, confident, kind, and a Warrior Unleashed. In fact, Stephanie was one of my mentors in fitness. When I was bone thin and wanted so badly to put on some muscle but terrified to go to the gym, she went with me and showed me how to workout. She taught me so much about fitness.

My sisters are my best friends who have influenced my life positively in so many ways. My older sister Sandra and I were so different growing up. She was a girly girl, and I was a tomboy so we didn't spend time hanging around together at school. But today Sandra and I are so alike and we talk nearly daily. Sandra is such a loving sweet person. She is like a pillar. A pillar of light, hope and strength for everybody that she loves. Especially her family and close friends. I can always count on Sandra to be right by my side during all the peaks and valleys of life. She is loyal to the core and I love her so much.

My youngest sister Irene and I were the most alike growing up and spent a lot of time together in our early 20's having fun and traveling together. Irene is the life of the party everywhere she goes including our family. She is full of smiles and knows how to not take life too seriously. I can always count on her to put things in perspective and to lighten the mood even on hard days. She brings so much joy into my life and to all that know her. She is beautifully anchored in her faith in the Lord, and is someone that I can count on for prayer daily. Irene is a prayer warrior for myself and many others. I am so grateful for my sisters and praise God for them every single day. My sisters are my ride or die, including my best friend Lisa who I consider a chosen sister.

I also adore my dogs Blaze and Journey and my cat Gunner–honestly, I believe animals are some of the most beautiful healing spirits. They sometimes feel like angels to me. I have been blessed with some of the most incredible friends and business partners. I'm obsessed with how to help people and animals, and that's what I get to spend all of my time doing. This is the life I set out to create, and this life leads to the legacy that lets me know I am giving it everything I have.

It is by design—day by day.

I think the mistake that can happen is that we don't realize the small daily actions create the big dream life. We might think, ugh, it's Monday afternoon, who cares it's not like one day can make a difference in the grand scheme of things. Maybe you let yourself off the hook and don't take the actions that could bring you closer to your goals. The problem isn't that you blew off working toward your goals for one Monday, it's that it happens for days on end, maybe even months or years. All the while, telling yourself you will start making a difference in your own life later. This is the accidental life, and sometimes it turns out fine, but for many, it just turns out far below what they had really wanted.

It's so important to have perspective and clarity about the big picture for yourself because it will inform what decisions you make on a day-to-day basis so, in the end, you have no regrets.

Jennifer K. Morgan

In reality, legacy is a daily activity, and this is a double-edged sword. On the one hand, if you have big goals, it's great to find out you reach them with small steps on a consistent basis over time. On the other hand, some people have a hard time not having instant gratification.

It's so much fun when something is just instantly gratifying, and that usually comes in the form of buying things, eating food, etc. I love fun as much as the next person, but here's what's not fun for me, trading in my goals and dreams (which add up to my legacy) for instant gratification.

In my perspective, I can't find gratification in anything that doesn't line up with what matters to me most. Being true to yourself is one of the healthiest and happiest decisions you can make. When I was younger, I struggled with people-pleasing, saying yes to things to make other people happy even if it wasn't in alignment with me.

Today, it's easy for me to decide what to say yes to, what to say no to, who and what to partner with because I'm clear on my end game. If an opportunity lines up with my end game, it's a yes, and if it doesn't, it's a no. It's so much more than business; it's your quality of life, your happiness. Happiness is a gift, and you deserve to be happy.

Here are 5 books I love that have all contributed to me gaining the tools I have today to create a legacy I'm proud of, and I thought I would share them with you:

1. The Bible is the ultimate personal development book. The Bible teaches us the importance of love and forgiveness, which are two of the greatest gifts of all. It also teaches us about perseverance, hope, faith, not to worry, not to fear, and to trust. It is the ultimate personal development book.

2. Rich Dad Poor Dad by Robert Kiyosaki was the first book I read that gave me my Aha moment on building a Big Business.

3. 5 Love Languages by Gary Chapman
When you learn what a person's love language is, you can create a better relationship with that person.

4. Think and Grow Rich by Napoleon Hill, this book orchestrates ways into the power of burning desire to change your mind and ultimately change your life.

5. 7 Habits of Highly Effective People by Stephen Covey This is an excellent book about self-motivation.

I can't encourage you enough to get crystal clear on what you want your legacy to be, and from that, reverse engineer the beliefs, behaviors, and actions to live your life without regret.

Chapter 5 Exercise

- What do you want your legacy to be? Write it down.

- If you vanished 10 minutes from now, what is your legacy? Write it down.

- Take a moment and evaluate what if anything, needs to be adjusted in your life to make sure you leave the legacy you want to leave?

- What actions do you need to take?

CHAPTER 6

Do the Right Thing

"Commit to the Lord whatever you do, and your plans will succeed."

Proverbs 16:13

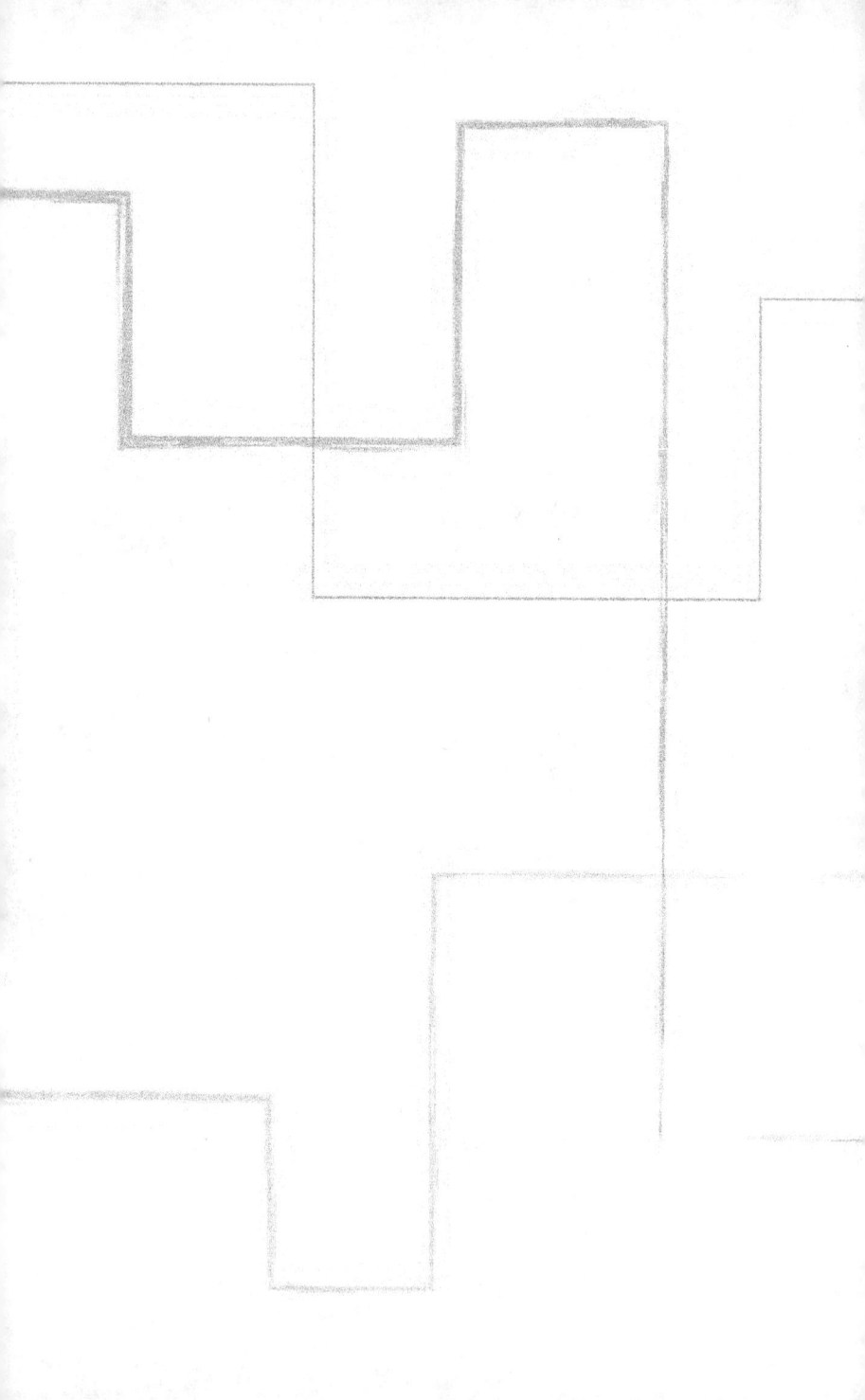

Do the Right Thing

"Commit to the Lord whatever you do, and your plans will succeed." - Proverbs 16:13

You can't go wrong doing the right thing. It sounds simple, but if it were, then everyone would be happy. The messy part about "right" and "wrong" is that they are subjective, in the eye of the beholder, so to speak. There are some clear lines that the masses agree on in terms of the law, for example. It's fairly cut and dry, don't run red lights, don't steal, don't injure another person, and so on. But what if you are running a red light because you're trying to rush someone to the hospital? What if you stole because your child was going to starve to death? What if you hurt someone in self-defense?

My point is that there is almost always another side to a story, and things can move from black and white to grey very quickly. In business and life, I have found that there are always many different ways to handle problems that arise, goals you want to achieve, and people in your life. We all get to define for ourselves what doing the "right thing" looks like and make decisions accordingly. I want to share with you what I have found over my lifetime of trial and error my metrics for doing the right thing, and they have never steered me wrong.

You can't go wrong doing the right thing.

Jennifer K. Morgan

If you have to step on anyone to get ahead, it's not the right thing.

Shortcuts are a misnomer when it comes to success. They imply there's a faster, easier way to get where you are trying to go, but the truth is they almost always set you back. I have seen it so often that I have to comment. I have seen people presented with an opportunity that will move a person forward but at the same time hold someone else back. I personally have had the opportunity to move ahead in my career that would have hurt other people, and I always found another way. Deep down, I knew that if I ever gained success by using someone else, it would NEVER feel like success to me. I have known people that said yes to shortcuts and hurt others along the way to achieve their success, and I know for sure those people could never shake the ugly feeling about how they got where they are, *how* they chose to get ahead siphoned the joy from the experience.

If you can't do it in the light, it's not the right thing.

Living a life of real freedom goes far beyond finances. Yes, having financial freedom can create a myriad of beautiful opportunities to choose from but if you say yes to anything you feel like you have to hide then it stops feeling like freedom. When we operate our businesses and lives in a way that we are truly proud of then, the sky's the limit on what you can accomplish and how great you will feel along the way. If I feel like there is any part of a deal that I can't move freely in the light with, then it's a hard and fast "no" for me. This is very personal and requires intentional introspection. If it feels off to you, then it doesn't matter if everyone around you gives you the green light, make your decisions based on what you can proudly and confidently share with the world.

If you can't be yourself, it's not the right thing.

This is a fixed guidepost for me. If I feel like I have to show up as anyone else besides myself to make a project successful, then it's not the right thing for me. There is nothing more isolating than feeling like you can't be yourself. You can be standing in a room full of people, and if you feel like you are saying things and acting in ways that are not authentic to you, you will feel alone. This also creates an enormous amount of stress inside of us. When our actions and words don't line up with what we are truly thinking and feeling, we experience duress. Psychology calls this cognitive dissonance. It's one thing to occasionally act happier than you feel, express more energy than you really have, or laugh at jokes that aren't funny. These short bursts of "faking" it are manageable, but if your life or business requires you to fake it for prolonged periods of time, you can become depressed, anxious, and miserable. Any opportunity or a friendship that you can't be you in is never the right thing.

Make your decisions based on what you can proudly and confidently share with the world.

Jennifer K. Morgan

Do the extraordinary thing when you can.

The right thing will keep everything internally and externally on the up, feeling good, and moving forward, which is a life well-lived. If you want to take it a step further, look for ways to do the extraordinary thing. The extraordinary thing is the decision that will help not only yourself win but others too. Look for ways to bring the greatest amount of value and service to yourself and as many others as possible inside of the same decision. The extraordinary thing brings everyone up, including yourself. Making decisions that keep you healthy and aligned with your purpose comes first because if there is no you then you have nothing to give. After you have figured out the best direction for you to go in, then ask yourself how could this also be of great service to others and how can I include that in my goals.

There are no problems that exist without a solution. Each of us serves a valuable and critical role in making this world a better place and this only becomes daunting if we believe we are alone. The reality is we are all individually responsible for our own journey. We each are the stewards of our own gifts and how we choose to share them. We cannot control anyone else beyond ourselves, so if each one of us does the right thing individually, we will save each other collectively. We really do rise together.

Let us not lose heart in doing good., for in due time we will reap if we do not grow weary. - Galatians 6:9

Chapter 6 Exercise

- Is there any area in your life that you feel like you can't be yourself that you'd like to change?

- If your answer is yes, what can you do to change it?

- Is there an opportunity for you to do the extraordinary thing?

- If you answered yes, write down your idea in detail and how you could begin to implement it.

CHAPTER 7

With or Without you

"But the Lord is with me like a mighty warrior."

Jeremiah 20:11

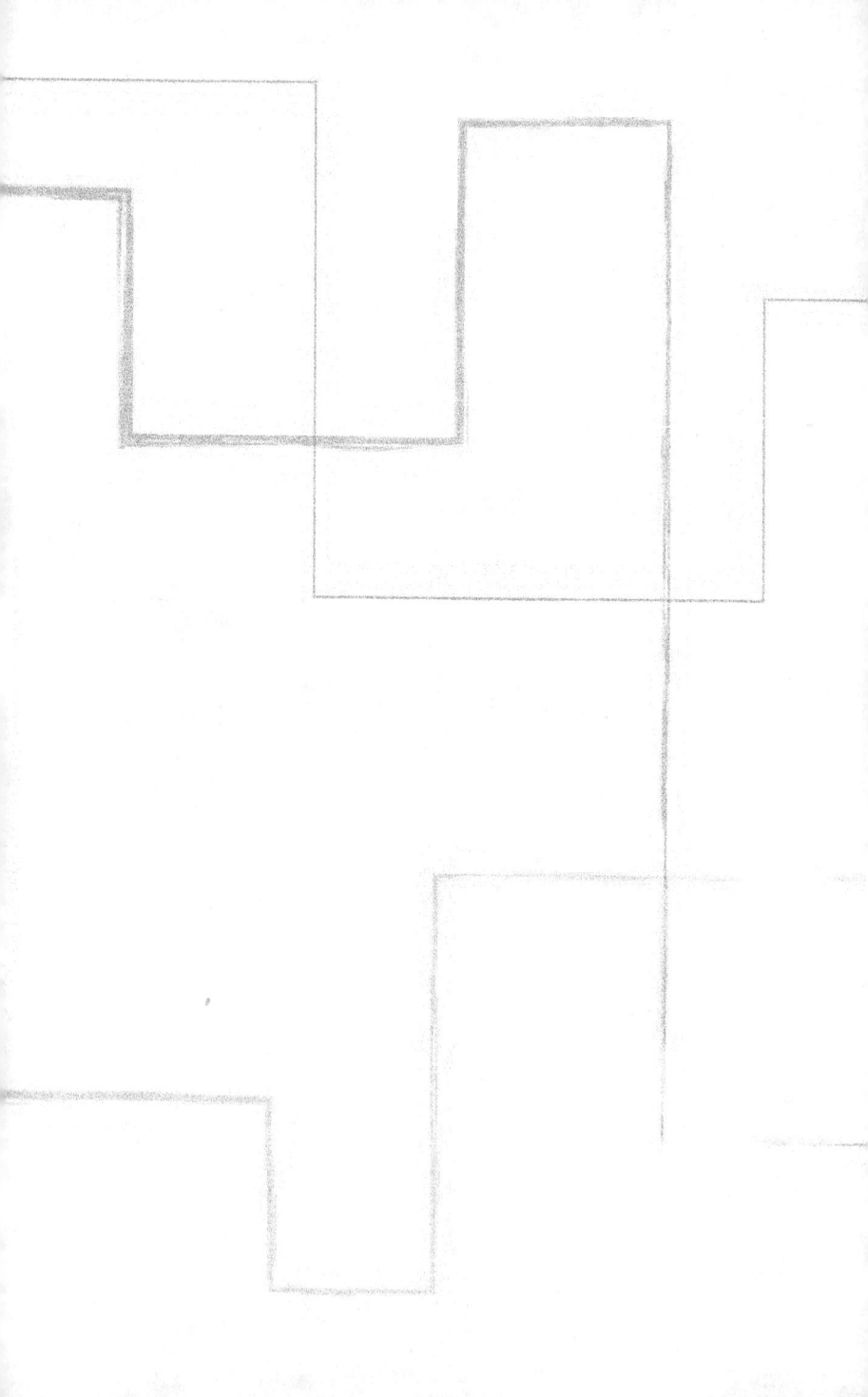

With or Without you

"But the Lord is with me like a mighty warrior"
- Jeremiah 20:11

When it comes to your goals or your dreams, you have to remember something essential, they are *your* goals and *your* dreams. You have to stay in the driver's seat no matter what. You have the vision for what you want to accomplish, and if you can see it, then it's possible. It's your road to take and your finish line to cross.

Have you ever shared a goal with someone, and they responded with something discouraging? Have you ever told someone what your dreams are, and they proceeded to tell you why it might not be possible to accomplish what you want? Often other people have good intentions when they list off to you what could go wrong and how it might not work. When this happens, they are sharing with you their own personal fears and perceived limitations for themselves. Your dreams and goals are not theirs even if they sound similar, you are unique and you get to decide what is too much or too little for you to handle. You have the grace and the grit built inside of you to accomplish your heart's desire and asking someone else if they think you should go for whatever it is you want to go for doesn't make sense.

You are the primary voice that matters in your head, and if you think you can do it, you can. The opposite is true as well, if you think you can't achieve something and everyone tells you that you can— it won't matter because the buck always stops with you. You have to take complete and total responsibility for making your dreams a reality. You are the one that wakes up with you every second of every day, you are the only one living your life no matter how many people you have around you. Our dreams and goals are our own responsibility and asking someone else if they are achievable is like driving your car with your eyes closed and asking a passenger to verbally guide you down the road. You are the one with your hands on the steering wheel, and it's your journey.

When you know what you want, you have to be willing to go *with or without* others. I call this having a W.O.W. attitude. When I set a goal, it is not contingent upon what someone else thinks is possible for me or if someone is willing to join me. I will do what I know I need to do with or without you.

You have to take complete and total
responsibility for making your dreams a reality.

Jennifer K. Morgan

A W.O.W. attitude isn't hurtful or stubborn as some might interpret, it's responsible and courageous. If you have ever decided to get in shape and had a workout or accountability partner you know that ultimately it's your job to get to the gym and work out, not your partners. What if your partner falls off the wagon and just starts sleeping in? Do you stop working out? If you are really taking responsibility for your own goals you show up for yourself, end of story.

What happens if you have a circle of friends or family members who you love and respect that don't want what you want out of life? What if what you want is so far out of their comfort zone that they feel like you are somehow leaving them by going to your desired next level? What if you lose people close to you because you are "changing" too much?

I learned a hard but necessary lesson: some people are meant to come with you, and some people you have to go forward without.

It has been said that we are the summation of the five people we hang around most. Take a moment to think about who you spend the majority of your time with? Are they living the life you dream of living? Do they challenge you? Are their dreams as big as yours, if not bigger? Do they feel like what you want out of life is more possible or less possible?

It's hard to ask ourselves these questions because we are afraid we might lose people. I have learned that the friends who are meant to stay will and the ones who aren't won't. My responsibility is to strive to be the best version of myself and take action toward what I believe is best for me that will help as many others as possible. If someone doesn't choose to join me on my journey then it's for the best.

If you want to make a difference in this world you can't be worried about making everyone happy.

1. It's impossible.

2. That's not your responsibility.

"So do not fear, for I am with you; do not be dismayed, for I am your God. I will strengthen you and help you; I will uphold you with my righteous right hand."
- Isaiah 41:10

As long as you are doing the right thing, as we talked about earlier, then you are on track for your best life. When you are aligned with the best version of yourself, and you take full responsibility for doing what it takes to live the best life you can, you won't lose. Playing small serves no one, you are here for a reason, and hiding out behind someone else's dreams or lack thereof won't cut it.

I have some dear life-long friends, Lisa and Greg, and they have shown up for me through every up and down. In fact, I consider Lisa my chosen sister; I have three incredible sisters by blood, but in spirit, I have four. When I have up-leveled, they are the first to celebrate with me, when I have felt stuck, they have been right there to problem-solve or encourage me, and when I've been at some of my lowest points, they are right there to pray with me or just listen.

Their dreams are as big as mine, if not bigger at times. They live the kind of life I enjoy living, and they are constantly looking for ways to grow and become even better. Those are my people. The tribe I choose has a growth mindset, they're real, and they have a W.O.W. attitude too.

The more clear and unapologetic you become about not just who you are but who you want to become, the easier it is to find your tribe. I love people with a W.O.W. attitude, they are on a mission, and they take action not because someone is making them but because that's who they are. They are the best people to team up with, be in business with, and do life with.

I have been in business a long time in diverse industries and have worked with more teams than I can even list, and consistently people with a W.O.W attitude would always rise to the top. I have split them into the three categories I went over in chapter 2: A-Player, B-Player, and C-Player.

A-Players have the W.O.W. attitude. They take full responsibility for reaching their goals. You won't ever hear them blaming others for why they aren't where they want to be yet. If there is a problem, they work on a solution not because someone told them to but because they saw a problem and knew it needed a solution.

A-Players go above and beyond and are willing to go the distance. You will often see A-Players as successful entrepreneurs, managers, or business owners.

B-Players do exactly what's required, no more and no less, and usually will need guidance. If you need something done, they will get it done, but if someone doesn't ask them to do it and it's not a part of their job description, they won't do it. They don't excel, but they also don't fail. However, I found many B-Players that are open and willing to be mentored and coached to become an A Player.

C-Players do just enough to not get fired or kicked off the team. They will seek out the bare minimum. Their goals are more food and shelter-based and less self-actualization in Maslov's Hierarchy of needs. You will not find them setting goals that will require them to take very much responsibility.

I am clear today that A-Players and some B-Players are my people and C-Players are not. I am selective about who I invest my time and energy into. I used to think that C-Players just needed some training and inspiration, and they would eventually become an A-Player, realizing how much more happy and successful they can be. No, not true, they drained me. People who don't take responsibility for their dreams and their well-being will inadvertently make others responsible. This creates a massive, uneven exchange of energy. I discovered how important it was for me to help people who want to help themselves. They would actually take what I had to give and multiply it in their lives. While others would take what I had to give, never apply it while continuing to stay stuck and complaining.

Chances are if you are reading my book, you have a W.O.W. attitude, and we are each other's people.

Chapter 7 Exercises

- Where in your life do you have a W.O.W. attitude?

- Are there any areas in your life that you feel you need to take more responsibility regarding the outcome?

- If yes, how could you begin taking more responsibility in gaining your desired outcome?

CHAPTER 8

Filling Your Cup

"May the God of hope fill you with all joy and peace as you trust in him, so that you may overflow with hope by the power of the Holy Spirit."

Romans 15:13

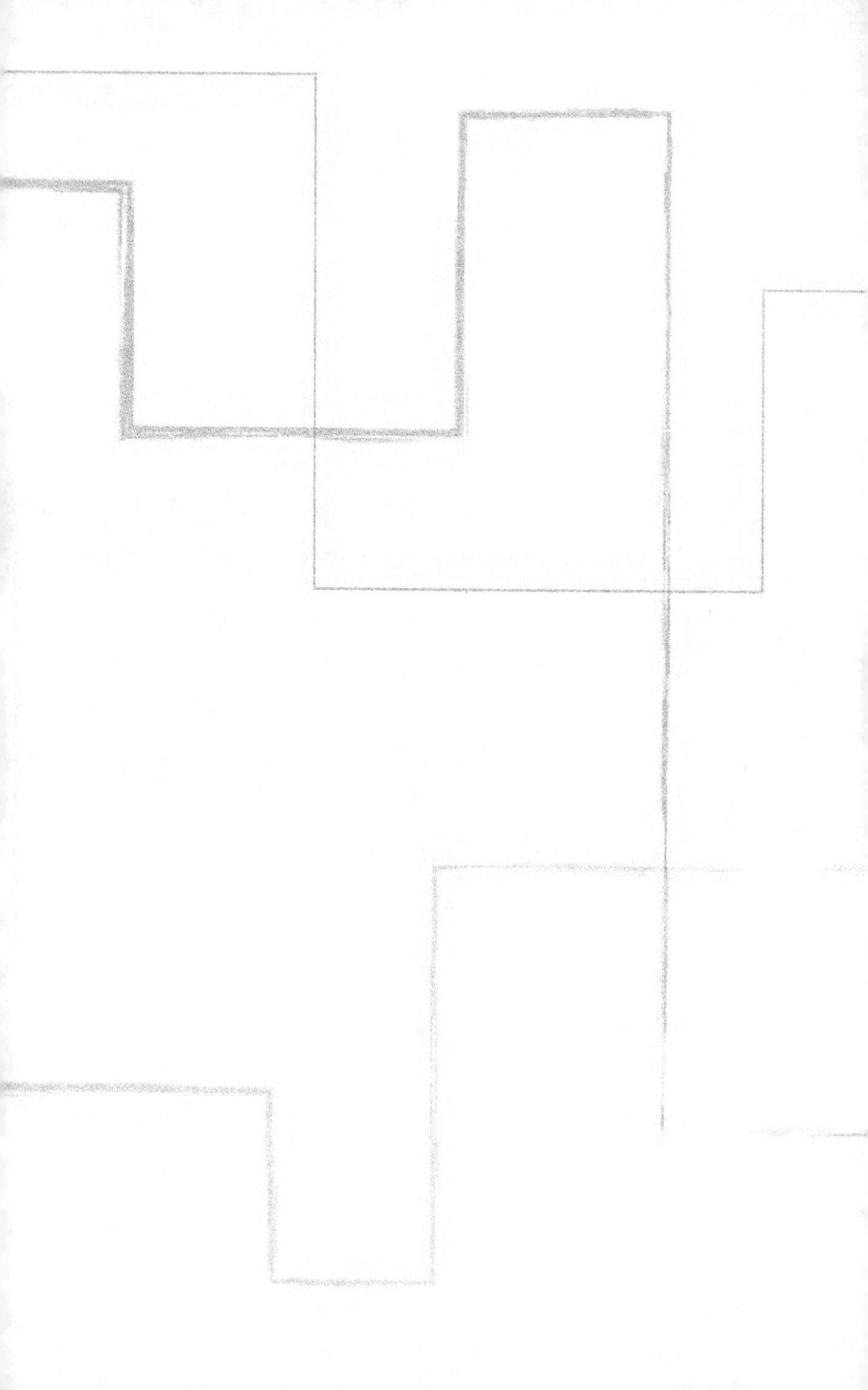

Filling Your Cup

'May the God of hope fill you with all joy and peace as you trust in him, so that you may overflow with hope by the power of the Holy Spirit.' - Romans 15:13

Living a life in service to others creates something bigger than yourself, significant, and deeply fulfilling, so it can be confusing when you hear that you have to put yourself first. But it's true, to be of great service in this world, you have to put yourself first. Rationally we know that if we are burnt out, sick, exhausted, overwhelmed, etc., it's nearly impossible to do our best. If someone is thirsty and we are holding an empty cup, we have no water to give.

We know this rationally, but somehow we still might find ourselves putting everyone's needs, wants, and desires before our own while we scrape by on fumes. Why do we do that? I've been there, and I've burned my candle and every candle I could find around me on both ends until I was completely burnt out and all in the name of wanting to help and make a difference.

I think we have to make the journey from the head to the heart on this one. We have to believe it in our heart that we are our greatest responsibility and worth caring for because when we do that, we can show up with our strongest, most vibrant self. This is such a powerful component to unleashing your inner warrior.

We make time for what we value most or perceive as the most critical demanding of our time, energy, and focus. When you look at your life, more specifically your days, how are you investing your time, energy, and focus? If you take inventory of everything from the time you wake up in the morning to when you fall asleep at night, you might find that YOU are hardly on your list if at all. Maybe the things you are doing are getting you closer to your goals which is fantastic but you might also be miserable getting there? This doesn't mean you need to change your goals, it just points to you needing to take care of yourself differently along the way.

If you find that you are burnt out, and you aren't even going in the direction you want to be going, you may need to step back and set new goals (which we go over in the next chapter), but this also indicates that your wellbeing hasn't made it on your to-do list.

This idea that it is selfish to put yourself at the top of your priority list is so destructive and ridiculous. If you were given one vehicle to drive for the rest of your life and that vehicle was the only way you could go anywhere, and that vehicle was literally your only connection to life as you know it, would you prioritize it? I'm sure it's an obvious yes.

> You are the only person that can prioritize your well-being.
>
> **Jennifer K. Morgan**

Our body, mind, and spirit are our vehicle, our ONLY vehicle here on earth to experience life, and yet we put ourselves last?

If you want to be able to be there for anyone or anything effectively, you have to put yourself at the top of your daily list. Taking care of yourself every once in a while is like showering every once in a while–it doesn't work--it's an everyday activity.

Taking care of yourself is not a luxury meant only for people with time to waste and money to spare, it's for humans who want to live and give and make their life count.

I think one of the main reasons people have a hard time prioritizing themselves in their own life is because no one is asking them to. Most people's time, energy, and focus are going to the places it's being requested or even demanded. Clients ask for your help, bosses ask for your help, your children ask for your help, your relationships ask for your help, your bills demand your attention, food and shelter demand your attention. The only person not asking you for anything is you, and you are the only person who can take care of you daily. You are the only person that can prioritize your well-being.

After working in health and wellness for several decades, I can say that many people see their health and wellbeing as optional until something catastrophic happens. They tell themselves that they just don't need that much sleep or don't have time. They are too tired to work out and too stressed and busy to eat healthily. Their mental stress is off the charts and express that they are too stressed and busy to relax. They get stuck in a cycle of an empty cup.

This is no way to live, and this leaves very little to give. So how do you get on your own priority list?

You put yourself on the list and view your wellbeing for what it is–the foundation your whole life rests upon.

First, prioritize the critical basics:

Sleep.

Are you getting enough sleep? Sleep is where all the magic happens. Your body and mind rest and regenerate. Sleep deprivation is one of the most effective forms of torture, worse than physical harm because, without it, we lose our physical and mental health. Sleep is one of the most valuable contributors to optimal health. Prioritize it. When you make your schedule, factor your bedtime in, not just your wake time. You may benefit from setting a nighttime alarm that signals it's time to turn off all of your devices and wind down for bed.

Water.

The only fluid that counts as water, in my opinion, is...water. If you're not drinking at least half your body weight in ounces each day, you're probably dehydrated. Water is the literal elixir of life, our bodies are comprised of 60% water. Every cell in the body depends on water, allowing them to grow, reproduce, and survive. The brain depends on water to manufacture neurotransmitters and hormones. The benefits of water could fill pages, but many don't realize the side effects of not drinking enough water: low energy, poor sleep, depressed mood, irritability, fatigue, digestive trouble, and of course, organs, tissues, and cells under-functioning. Increasing your water intake is often one of the most overlooked yet easiest ways to elevate your sense of wellbeing.

Joy

Joy isn't something you wait for to pop up out of nowhere. It's something you intentionally make space for in your life on a daily basis, at least it can and should be. According to the APA Dictionary of Psychology, joy is a feeling of extreme gladness, delight, or exultation of the spirit arising from a sense of well-being or satisfaction. The feeling of joy may take two forms: passive and active. Passive joy involves tranquility and a feeling of contentment with things as they are. Active joy involves a desire to share one's feelings with others. It is associated with more engagement of the environment than is passive joy. The distinction between passive and active joy may be related to the intensity of the emotion, with active joy representing the more intense form. Both forms of joy are associated with an increase in energy and feelings of confidence and self-esteem. Joy can be found in small things that don't take a lot of time. Make a list of what brings you joy and schedule it inside of your day.

> "Joy is not necessarily the absence of suffering, it is the presence of God."

Sam Storms

It could be a 5-minute walk outside. Spending time in prayer. Drinking a cup of tea or coffee from your favorite place. Reading a few pages of a book you've wanted to read. Spending quality time with your loved one or spouse. Playing with your children or your pets. Watching the sunrise or set. Do at least one thing every day that brings you joy, even if you don't feel like it at first. You will begin to notice almost right away how powerful the practice of putting yourself first to create space in your life is, and it will overflow into the rest of your day.

Filling your cup is another gift that keeps on giving. When you make time for taking care of yourself, it's almost like time expands for you. You may think you're too busy or tired, but I can promise you that if you put yourself at the top of your priority list, you will have more energy, less stress, better health, and so much more. You are so valuable, and what you have to offer matters so much.

Chapter 8 Exercise

- Do you feel like your wellbeing is one of the most important things in your life? If not, why?
- Make a list of how you are currently filling your cup.
- Make a list of the ways you could make yourself a higher priority in your life and schedule what you come up with.

CHAPTER 9

Life on Purpose

"Before I formed you in the womb I knew you, before you were born I set you apart; I appointed you as a prophet to the nations."

Jeremiah 1:5

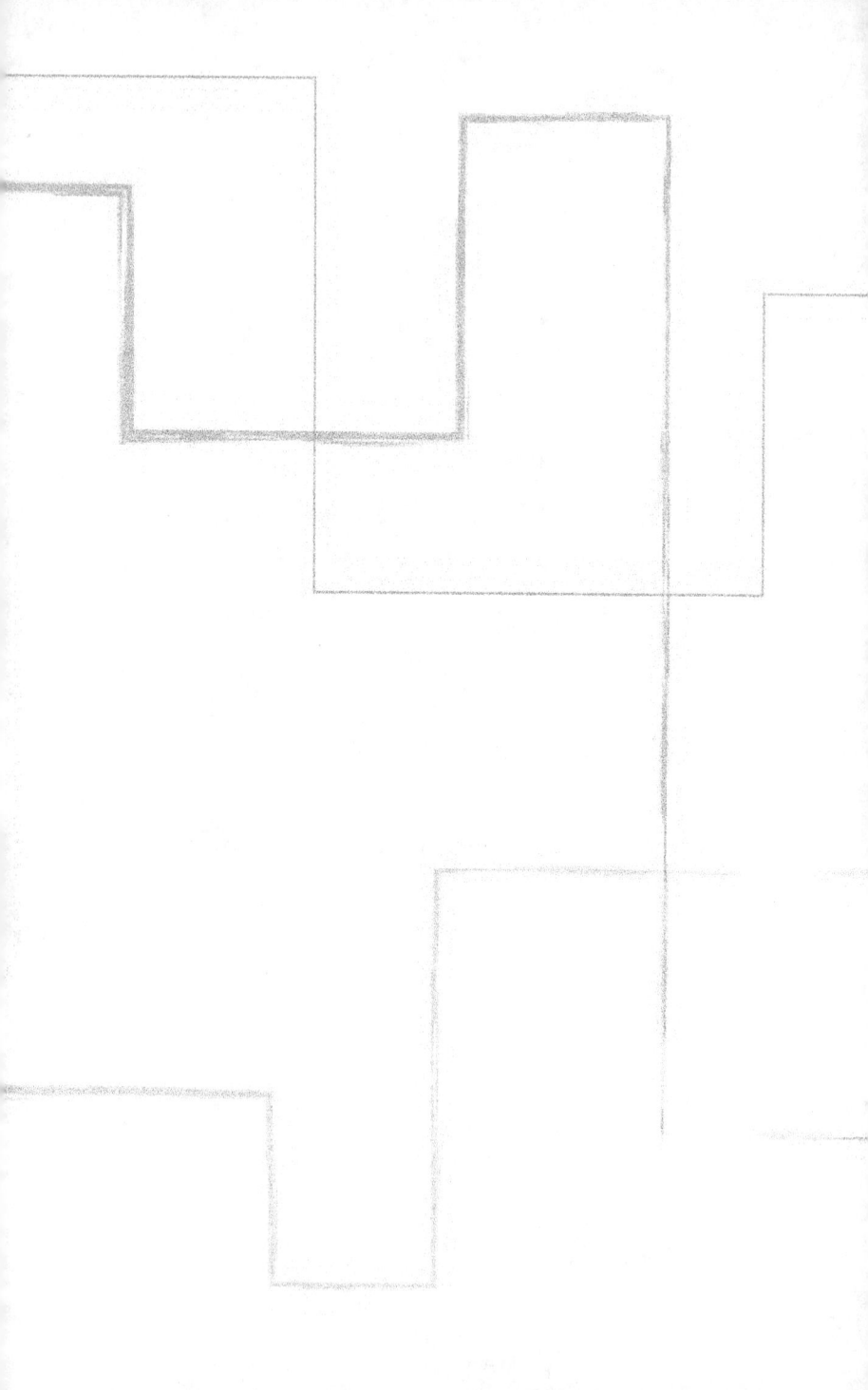

Life on Purpose

"Before I formed you in the womb I knew you, before you were born I set you apart; I appointed you as a prophet to the nations." - Jeremiah 1:5

I know what it's like to wake up in the morning and dread the day ahead because it's filled with things that leave you feeling tired and unfulfilled. So when I share that I feel blessed because from an early age, something inside me understood that I have a purpose, and I needed to live out whatever that purpose is, know that it doesn't mean I haven't been through hell and back. However, understanding that I had a purpose did wonders for me because it practically made me allergic to doing things that felt off-purpose. If I said yes to a project, partnership, friendship, opportunity, etc., and woke up with a pit in my stomach, my internal, off-purpose alarm system would begin to sound. This was great because in retrospect I couldn't travel too far in the wrong direction because the alarm inside would be yelling "wrong direction Jen! Reroute!" I realize not everyone has such a strong reaction to feeling off-purpose, at least that they're aware of consciously.

Legacy happens either by default or design. Legacy by design happens when you decide in advance what you want to see when you look back on your life and what you want to leave behind.

Jennifer K. Morgan

I believe we really do all have a purpose and that when we are living on purpose, it unlocks the very best of us. We have our best ideas and the determination to see them through. We connect with others more readily and authentically. When we live on purpose, I think it makes us want to run toward life and not be away from it.

Living on purpose is conscious and intentional, requiring us to stay in manual and out of autopilot. Some might argue that this sounds like more work, but I assure you it's not. Living on autopilot creates more stress and energy loss than we can imagine. When we are living off purpose, keeping our heads above water is a full-time 24/7 day week job. Whether we are aware or not, some part of us understands we're made for more. This creates a void. No amount of accolades, financial wins, compliments, etc., can fill the void of feeling purposeless.

You know you're on purpose when you wake up in the morning, and you feel like getting out of bed and fully engaging in your life. Things are going *really* well when you can't wait to get out of bed because you are so excited about your life, what you do for a living, the people you spend time with, the relationships in your family, and where you're headed.

Living on purpose is part of putting yourself first. When you take care of yourself and prioritize what is best for you, living on purpose comes naturally. If you give yourself permission to be yourself and be honest about what truly matters to you, your purpose reveals itself through your heart's desires. Your true nature lines up with what your gifts are, and the more you lean into what comes naturally to you, the more effective you will become.

I love helping people hit their goals, dream big, and live life to their fullest potential. Nearly every "job" I've had throughout my life has given me the opportunity to do that. In health and fitness, when I co-owned a gym and gave 110% to build up my staff and build up my clients. Every company I have worked with, I got to breathe as much life as possible to my team and thousands of clients. It's what I do with my friends and my family.

What I do for a living is an extension of who I am, and I designed it that way. I love waking up and knowing I am living on purpose. No matter how badly I have slept or how much pain my body is in from RA, my spirit is fulfilled even if I feel physically and mentally bereft at times. You might feel like your job is just something you suffer through to support your life, but when you do the math, you spend a significant amount of your time and energy working. Investing large amounts of our life in anything we feel off-purpose with can be devastating.

If you don't like your job, you don't necessarily have to quit. Sometimes there are changes we can make right where we are that can make an enormous difference. Take a look at what you do for a living and evaluate if there is anything you can integrate into your work that would get you living more on purpose? Is there an area that could use your skillset that you would love to contribute to? Are there people that could use some extra encouragement? Look at your work with fresh eyes and see how you could show up with more of yourself and more on purpose.

When we live on purpose, I think it makes us want to run toward life and not be away from it.

Jennifer K. Morgan

If you have been considering doing something new for a living but have been nervous about making the change, maybe it's time to put some timelines on your goals and take action. Trust that what is inside of you is ready and wants to come out. Become the warrior unleashed and do what needs to be done.

Trust me, inside of you is a bold, powerful, loving, courageous, compassionate warrior that knows what to do and won't let you down. She was handcrafted and chosen for such a time as this by a God that loves her fiercely and will always have her back. She is you, and you have a purpose.

> *"She is clothed with strength and dignity, and she laughs without fear of the future." - Proverbs 31:25*

Chapter 9 Exercise

- Describe in detail what you living on purpose looks and feels like.

- Do you believe that you are living on purpose? Take a minute to free-write your thoughts and see what comes up.

- Are there any changes you have felt that you'd like to make in your life, but you've been afraid to make them?

- How will your life benefit by you making those changes?

- What are you risking by not making those changes?

CHAPTER 10

Do the Hard Thing

"Do not be anxious about anything, but in everything, by prayer and petition, with thanksgiving, present your requests to God. And the peace of God, which transcends all understanding, will guard your hearts and your minds in Christ Jesus."

Philippians 4:6-7

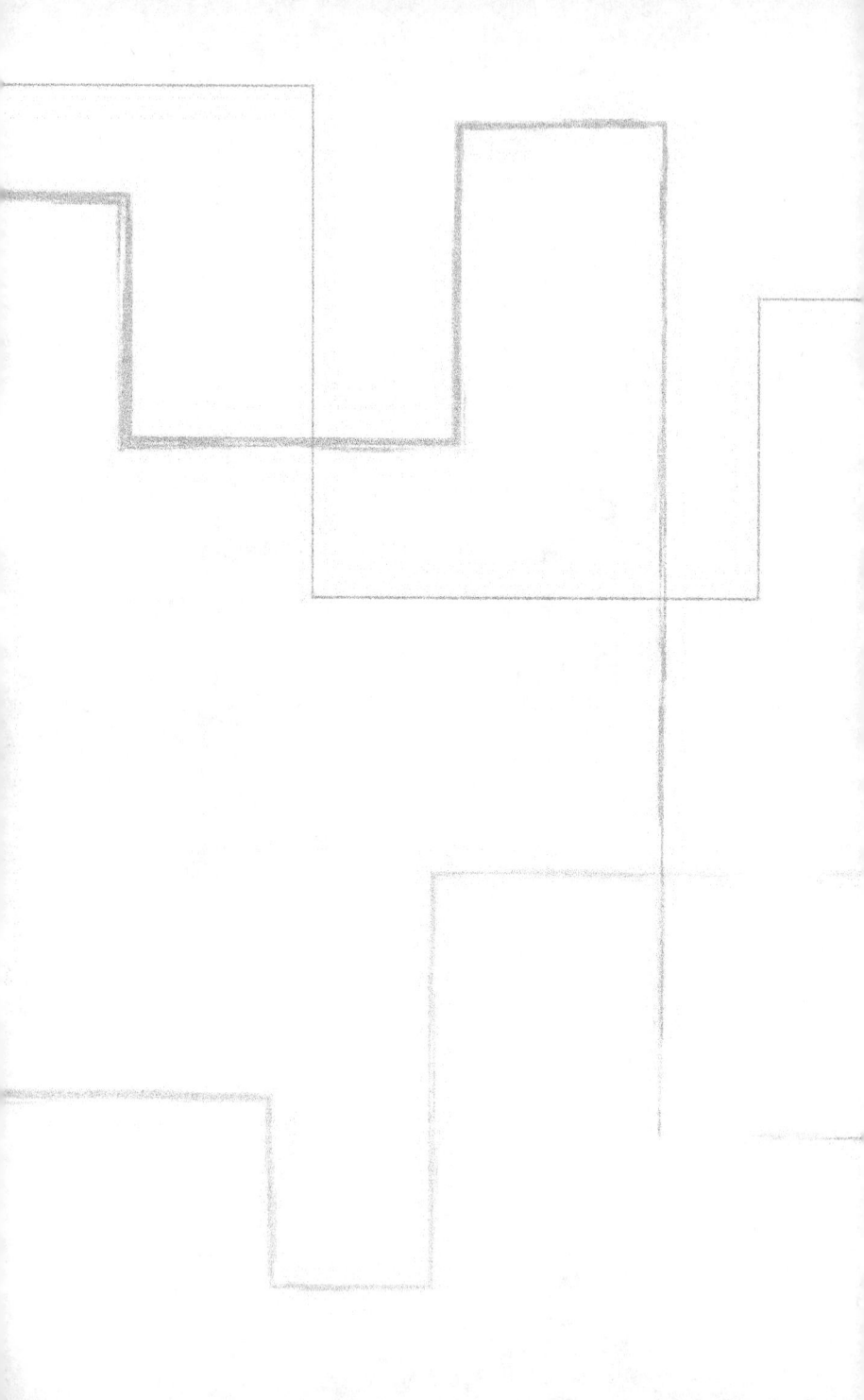

Do the Hard Thing

"Do not be anxious about anything, but in everything, by prayer and petition, with thanksgiving, present your requests to God. And the peace of God, which transcends all understanding, will guard your hearts and your minds in Christ Jesus" (Philippians 4:6-7).

Do it. DO the dream. It's fun to think about what could be, to imagine the possibilities and how amazing things would be if they became your reality. It's powerful to dream. Seeing what you want in your mind is strategically the first step to building the kind of life you feel is on purpose and will leave a legacy. The next step from dreaming is *doing*. Action is where people get stuck because the action is the hard thing or at least is perceived as the hard thing.

I lean into the hard thing, the action, especially the parts that I want to do the least. It may seem counterintuitive, but it's not; it can be your secret weapon that brings you the most amount of success. There are literally endless opportunities that are accessible to anyone who is willing to take action. Unfortunately, the vast majority of people don't want to do the hard thing.

I have experienced a lot of loss throughout my life of people I loved. I lost one of my closest friends when I was only 16 years old. She was killed in a car accident. She had asked me to skip school and just have a day of fun the day she passed. My parents were really strict, and I was certain they would lose their mind if I ditched class, so I very reluctantly didn't join her in the car that day. When I learned of her death that night, I was heartbroken, and it also scared me to my core. So much so that I didn't get my driver's license until I was 23 years old. Even then, it was only because the guy I was dating at the time gave me an ultimatum, get my driver's license, or he would break up with me. I think it was because he understood I was stuck in fear due to the trauma of losing my friend. He was probably also sick of driving me around. Either way, he knew he had to get me unstuck, and it worked. I am grateful to him today for that push. I was so afraid, but I forced myself to go in and take the test. It may sound trivial to some that I had such a debilitating fear of driving, but you may be able to relate if there has ever been anything that scares you to death, so you find yourself avoiding it at all cost, even if it would be good for you.

It's powerful to dream.

Jennifer K. Morgan

I was also terrified of public speaking. Just the thought of it would give me that sick feeling of nervousness in my stomach, but I hit a point in my career where I was being asked to speak often in front of team members in my companies and in front of several thousand on stage. I remember the first time I was asked to speak in front of a very large audience, and the fear was nearly paralyzing. I had a decision to make; either I was going to push through and grow, or I needed to accept the limitation I had set for myself—my desire to be of service and grow won. I practically blacked out when I held the mic, starring at all of the faces staring back at me, I was convinced everybody in the audience could see my heart beating through my chest, but I did it. And I have kept doing it, and it has become easier and easier because I was determined to do the hard thing.

Doing what's hard can bring up all the fear and uncertainty that you have around making your dreams come true, at first. When your dreams and the goals you have that will bring your dreams to life are safely nestled away in your mind, there is no risk of failure. I believe the fear of failure is the desert people don't want to cross to get to the promised land. When you cross the desert of uncertainty, all of the negative what-ifs arise: *What if you're not good enough? What if you're not smart enough? What if you don't know enough? What if you fail?* The what-ifs are endless. So people stay where they are, pacing the edge of the desert, dreaming about their dreams but terrified to take action. They stay stuck, stuck in fear.

Part of doing the hard thing is being willing to think about the hard things. Ask the hard questions and hang around long enough in the discomfort to get a real answer. Let's do it now together.

What are you afraid of?

If you can learn to look fear in the eye and do it anyway, you become virtually unstoppable. Your inner warrior is fully equipped to handle even seemingly insurmountable challenges; you just have to master moving beyond your fear. Identifying what your afraid of can help pull the rug out from under the power, you believe it has over you. So again, what are you afraid of?

Failure? If you're afraid you might fail, I'd like to share how I deal with my fear of failing. Failing is learning. I want to learn, I see it as a fundamental stepping stone to hitting my goals. Failing is a practical and necessary part of succeeding because I can't succeed if I'm unwilling to learn. When that little voice comes up in me and whispers, "What if you fail, Jen?" Then my answer is, "Then I'll learn, and it will only bring me that much closer to my goals." I'm willing to fail because I'm determined to succeed.

Are you afraid you're not enough? Smart enough? Knowledgeable enough? I am going to share a little secret. Everyone has felt this way, including me and everyone who has done anything great. Basically, it's a sign of courage. The only people who get hit really hard with these questions of self-doubt are the ones pushing past their comfort zone. If you keep your world really small and the same as it's always been, then you have nothing to fear. When there's nothing new to learn, you mitigate the chance of failure, and you don't question your enoughness because you don't have to challenge yourself in any way. If you have the courage to go beyond your comfort zone, you can expect to have some feelings of self-doubt come up. Here is the great news: the cause is the cure in this case. The feelings of self-doubt come up because you're afraid and moving into uncharted territory, but the further along you go, the self-doubt becomes less and less. If you give yourself the chance despite your fears of doing the hard thing, you will discover what we all do: you may not know everything but you do know how to figure it out as you go.

If you can learn to look fear in the eye and do it anyway, you become virtually unstoppable.

Jennifer K. Morgan

My Friend, I'll put it to you like this, if your dreams don't scare you a little, they aren't big enough, and if you don't fail on occasion, you're not trying hard enough. Ironically, trying to avoid fear creates more fear. You become afraid of being afraid, and on top of that, your dreams fall to the wayside.

Not doing the hard thing doesn't make life easy it makes life painful. If you go all-in on your dreams, face your fears, and simply don't give up on taking every action necessary, you will eventually make it to the life you've been dreaming about. It's hard, but there is a massive payoff, and that payoff can positively affect countless people and continue to do so for generations. But if you spend your life pacing on the edge of the desert trying to safeguard yourself from fear, your dreams will never come true. Your legacy might be, "I did my best with the little amount of rope I gave myself, and I never knew failure, but I never knew success either." That to me doesn't sound hard, it sounds devastating. Doing the hard thing by facing my fears and putting in the hard work has always been my strategic advantage. I've always been willing to do whatever it takes.

One of the character traits that I'm eternally grateful for from my parents is my work ethic. I am not afraid of hard work. My parents taught me by example that if you are willing to work hard, you will never be without, and you can hit your goals. I carried it everywhere I went from a very young age. I would set a goal, work hard by taking action until I achieved my goal. If hitting my goal required 300 phone calls, I made 300 phone calls. If I needed to wake up early and stay up late, then so be it. It never crossed my mind that I could achieve my goals in any other way than being willing to do the work, and further, I was taught that you never quit until the job is done.

I know we can make it complicated and painful and drag our goals across decades, but that's not how I do it, and I want you to know you don't have to do it that way either. No matter how much time you feel you've wasted or how scared you are, you can literally change it today by setting your goals and doing the work starting right now. Let's do the hard thing now so we can have the best thing later.

Chapter 10 Exercise

- Name 3 hard things you have been avoiding that would make your life better if you just did them.

- Why have you not already done them?

- If you do the 3 hard things you named, how will your life be better?

- If you don't do the 3 hard things you named, how will your life be worse?

- If you are willing to do the hard things you listed above, write down the date you will get these things done by_____.

CHAPTER 11

A New Kind of Health

'The LORD is my shepherd, I lack nothing.
He makes me lie down in green pastures,
he leads me beside quiet waters,
he refreshes my soul. He guides me along
the right paths for his name's sake.
Even though I walk through
the darkest valley, I will fear no evil,
for you are with me; your rod
and your staff, they comfort me."

Psalm 23:1-4

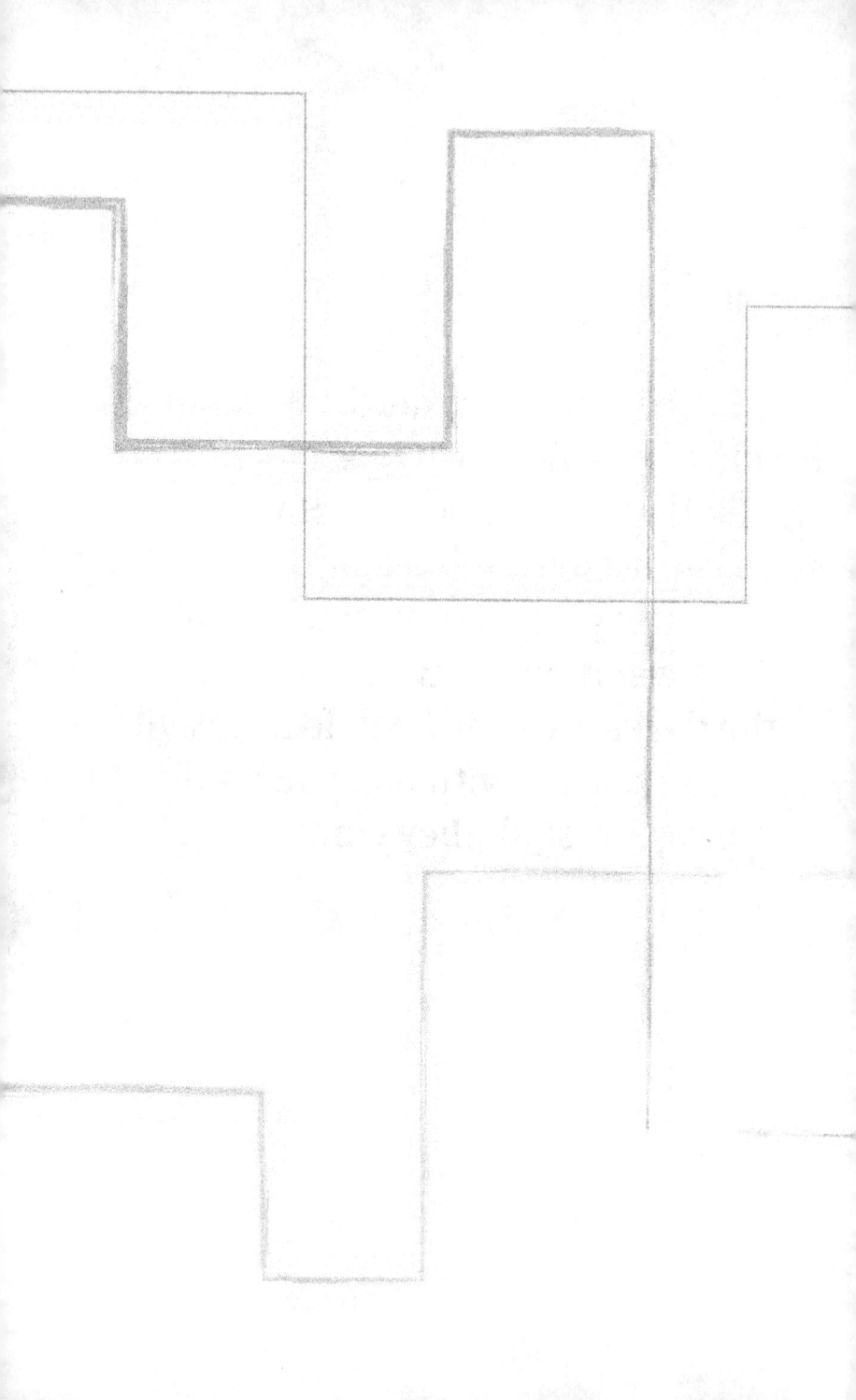

A New Kind of Health

'The LORD is my shepherd, I lack nothing. He makes me lie down in green pastures, he leads me beside quiet waters, he refreshes my soul. He guides me along the right paths for his name's sake. Even though I walk through the darkest valley, I will fear no evil, for you are with me; your rod and your staff, they comfort me.' -Psalm 23:1-4

My understanding of health has evolved and expanded tremendously with each passing level (I call each birthday a "new level"). It's so much more fun this way. My health journey began at 18 when I found fitness as a solution for me to put on muscle. As I mentioned earlier, I would wear two pairs of jeans in high school just to appear less thin. Weight training not only helped me change my body, my body became strong; it made me feel sexy, strong, and empowered. I had felt painfully insecure for years about how my body looked and had been made fun of so often that I just wanted to hide. Fitness gave me a new confidence and a sense that I could do anything. I woke up early and would train hard, eat healthily, and I would meet the day with so much energy. I loved it so much it became part of my career.

My journey as an entrepreneur officially took off when I found health. When I met Dr. Chet Graham, my previously mentioned mentor, who heavily influenced my desire to gain a much deeper understanding of not only business but nutrition and peak performance. He introduced me to the world of micronutrition, optimal macro nutrition and showed me how it positively impacts the body and mind when balanced. He really taught me the importance of gut health and using food and vitamins in place of medicine or integratively if needed. Gaining his insights opened my mind to a whole new level of health and gave me the courage to go big in business. When I said yes to co-owning a Golds Gym in my early 30s, I knew that his mentorship had played a significant role in saying yes to the opportunity.

Health and business were love at first sight for me. They gave me what I value most in life, freedom. Health is the air, and business is the airplane that has allowed me to travel across the world, meet the most incredible people, and help my loved ones and people from all walks of life gain freedom of their own design.

> Whole health is comprised of my body, mind, and spirit.
>
> Jennifer K. Morgan

Along the way, I discovered a new kind of health beyond the physical paradigm I had held in my formative years. Whole health is comprised of my body, mind, and spirit. When I was diagnosed with Rheumatoid Arthritis (RA), I had already gone through several years prior where I knew something was wrong. My energy had rapidly declined, I was in pain that continued to increase, and working out as I had before was impossible. As I shared, this was terrifying to me. My physical health was so much more than an aesthetic and career. I felt my freedom was suddenly hanging in the balance.

With my body going through a severe crisis, my mind and spirit had to come to the rescue. I became vigilant about what my thought life consisted of and completely committed to my faith in God. If you had asked me before living with RA the status of my thought life and faith, I would have said they were great. However, when my physical health was coming to what appeared to be a screeching halt, both my thoughts and faith wanted to run headlong into the fear, and frankly, no one would have blamed me. I had to dig deeper than ever before to stay in the driver's seat of my life. When you hear the words "there is no cure" and "drastic lifestyle change" and "long-term medical pain management," it knocks the air out of you. Feelings of hopelessness would be a natural next step, and feeling somehow abandoned by God would also be understandable. But the still small voice inside me said *there is so much more in you and for you here, have faith.* **Your test will become your testimony are words that echoed daily in my mind.**

I have always felt I had a warrior spirit but having RA unleashed her entirely. I knew that I was not alone in my battle with RA, I also knew it would somehow be used for good if I let it. My thought life has never been more vibrant and focused on what's possible and solution-oriented. I refuse to dwell on thoughts that bring me down. My health literally depends on it. When I focus on what *I can do* and who *I can help*, I feel healthy even if I'm in physical pain. My relationship with God has become the most profoundly satisfying part of my existence. We talk from the time I get up to the moment I fall asleep. I have never experienced the peace and joy that I have today.

Further, my businesses have hit a level of financial freedom that has set us up for generations, and I just keep thinking of new and creative ways for me to serve using the things that I have learned. My long-standing merchandise line, for example, called the Spirited Sparrow is filled with items that inspire me and others online. My husband Steve and I are preparing to launch Jewells Legacy Foundation, our nonprofit dedicated to helping dogs and cats in need and Military Veterans. Both of which are near and dear to our hearts. My husband Steve and I have never been closer or happier together than we are now. I take nothing for granted. I have committed to contributing to the conversation about thriving, even with RA because 1.3 Million people in America alone have Rheumatoid Arthritis (RA).

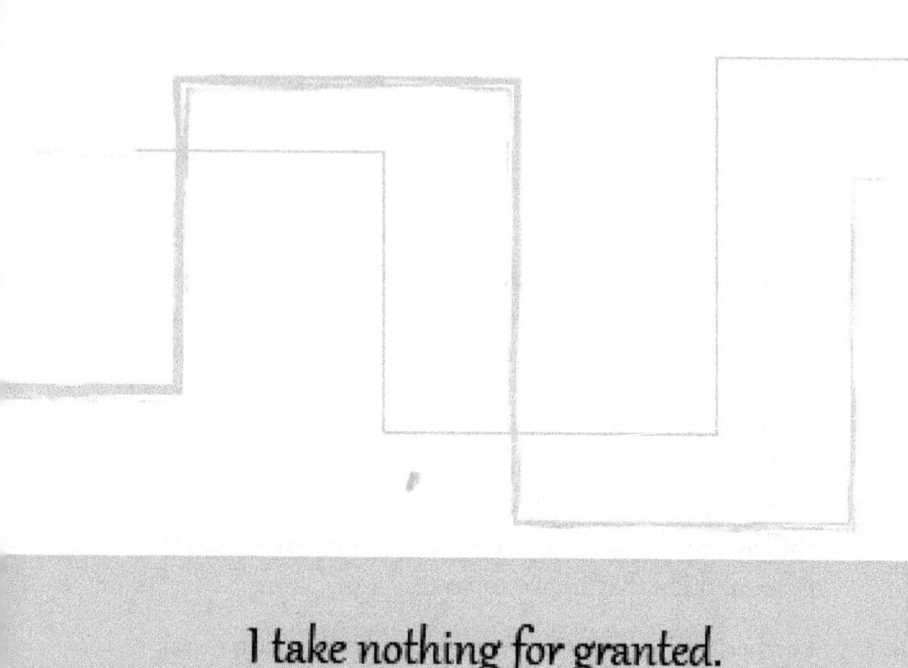

I take nothing for granted.

Jennifer K. Morgan

I have continued to take part in some very innovative and heavily researched therapies that are showing great promise with reducing the symptoms of the RA and moving me closer to remission. What I find most remarkable is that if you would have asked me if I could be free without my full physical health, I would have said no but here I am feeling freer than ever before. Facing possibly my greatest fear has shown me that my health is so much more than just my body, that I am the happiest when I am contributing to something bigger than me, and I have never known the peace and joy that I have today from nourishing my soul with my conversations with God. If you fear that losing something in this life will take away your freedom, purpose, legacy, or what brings you joy then it's not really freedom. I think I'm truly free for the first time.

We are resilient, purposeful, unique, powerful souls that have come to fully live these lives we've been given.

Let nothing stop you from dreaming your biggest dreams, contributing to something bigger than yourself, connecting with a God who loves you, leaving a legacy that matters to you, doing the right thing, believing in yourself no matter what, unapologetically taking care of yourself first so you've got something left to give, living a life of purpose by doing what you love, doing the hard things so you can create what you meant to create here and know that your freedom can not be given or taken away by something outside of yourself.

You came here for a reason, I believe we all have and I pray you believe in yourself as much as I do. I am a warrior unleashed and I am joining hands with my tribe– may we continue to powerfully move forward together.

God Bless You- Jen

Let's stay connected!

www.jenniferkmorgan.com

www.ingramcontent.com/pod-product-compliance
Lightning Source LLC
Chambersburg PA
CBHW070157100426
42743CB00013B/2952